Welcome to the team!

SAVE YOUR PAPER...

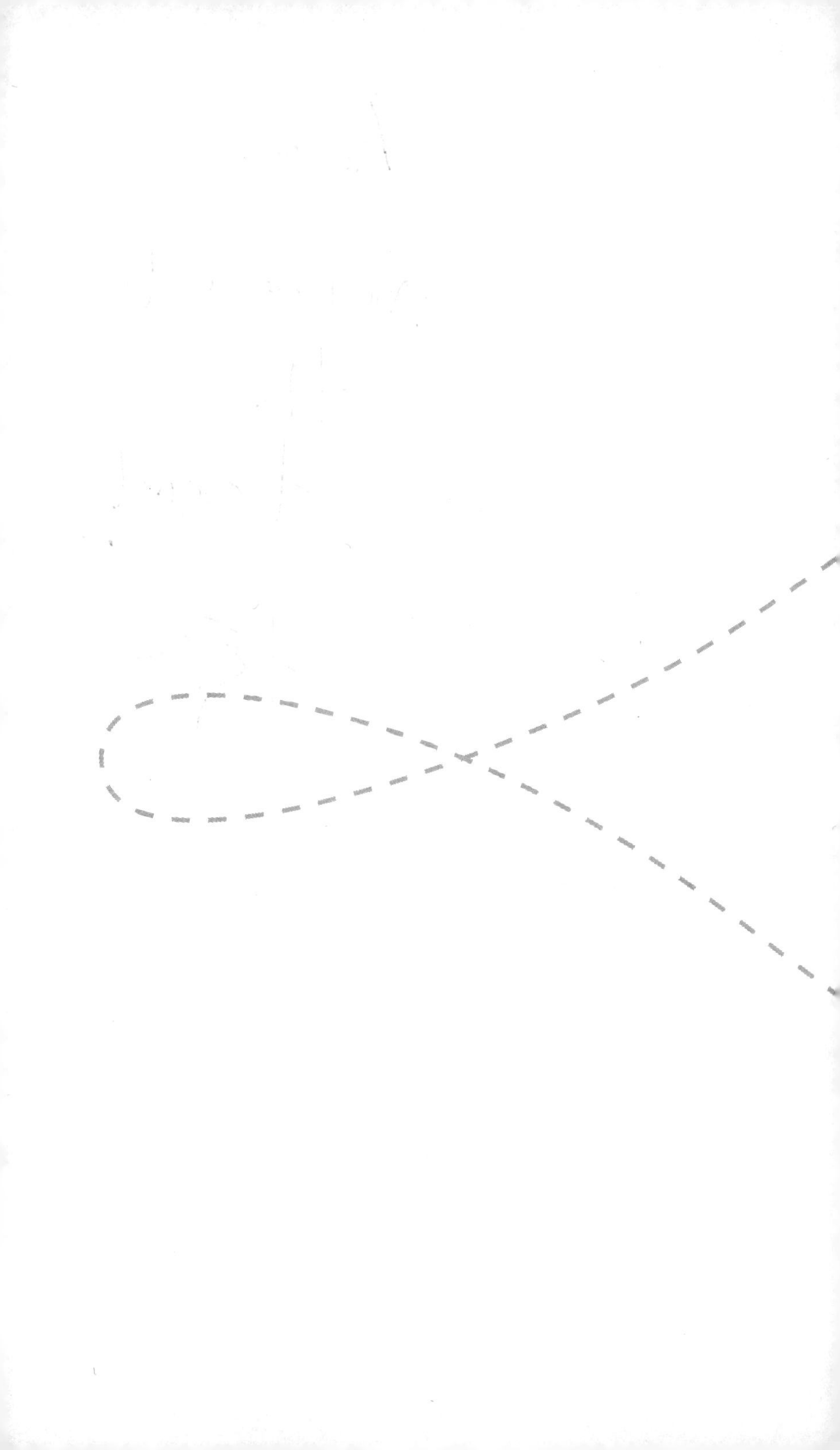

...FOR PAPER AIRPLANES.

SkySlope, Inc.

"SkySlope is the Apple of paperless platforms."

Mike Zagaris, President/CEO, *PMZ Real Estate*

"SkySlope adapts its online world to how brokers run their deals...The biggest reason we switched to SkySlope was its usability and high adoption rate."

Larry Matos, President, *Century 21 M&M*

"We looked at other systems but decided on SkySlope because a skilled real estate agent designed it for use by other agents. SkySlope has a user-friendly interface so it's not scary."

Glenn "Chip" Gardner, VP of Special Initiatives, *Gardner, Realtors®*

"I had used a competing transaction management platform for a couple of years before turning to SkySlope. SkySlope serves us better...The 24/7 support services at SkySlope relieve approximately two hours a day of interruptions of my auditing staff from agents asking questions."

Stacy Hall, Broker/Partner, *Keller Williams*

"Aside from its simplicity of use, one of the leading factors in choosing SkySlope was that an actual real estate agent created it, someone from within our industry. So SkySlope was developed from direct experience with agents' daily need to make more efficient use of their time...SkySlope is definitely a big advantage in attracting and retaining high-performing agents."

Dale Milton, Broker/Owner, *DPR Realty*

"With our previous online system, I had to have IT people on staff to field support questions. SkySlope' support team is there 24/7...SkySlope's team is top notch and very professional."

Matthew Crumbaugh, President, *Allison James Estates & Homes*

"What impressed me about SkySlope was that it clearly understood real estate transactions from a practitioner's viewpoint...And SkySlope conformed to our company's methods of handling transactions."

J. Scott Leonard, President/CEO, *Guarantee Real Estate, a Berkshire Hathaway Affiliate*

Contents

Acknowledgment

Introduction

1 **Freedom From the Burden of Paperwork** 3

'I loved working' 4

What changed my life 6

Dipping my toes in real estate 9

Ramping up my potential 12

'A mountain of paperwork' 14

'Built by and for agents and brokers' 18

2 **SkySlope's Unique Advantage: Customized to Fit Each Broker's Business** 25

Connecting the platform to the brokers 26

Building out the broker's side 28

Beefing up SkySlope to meet brokers' needs 32

Customizing SkySlope for each individual broker 37

Saving money and staying compliant 44

Differences between SkySlope and its competitors 47

Unique culture yields innovation & productivity 60

3 **SkySlope: Built by Agents for Agents** 71

No more trekking to the office to drop off or pick up 74

Making it easier for agents to respond 83

Companies that think they're paperless, but aren't 85

It's painless to go paperless 90

About Tyler Smith 93

Acknowledgements

I'd like to dedicate this book to all the agents and brokers whose ideas and suggestions have helped shape SkySlope into what it is today. Without their contributions, SkySlope wouldn't have been able to evolve from a single-user platform into the platform that it is now, serving top agents and brokers across the nation.

Also, I'd like to thank Marc Grossman, who helped me mold my thoughts and words so that I could share SkySlope's story.

TYLER SMITH

"As we express our gratitude, we must never forget that the highest appreciation is not to utter words, but to live by them."

—President John F. Kennedy

Introduction

Leading both agents and brokers into the future of real estate.

As a highly successful real estate agent, I needed something to help me overcome the crushing burden of paperwork—so I created SkySlope. Now this vision is paving the way for the future of real estate by transforming companies' workflows from paper to paperless.

We've all seen real estate agents hunched over, lugging around heavy briefcases with transaction folders, sometimes on wheels, that they need to access quickly. My team and I were no different. By 2009, when I was a practicing Realtor®, we were selling hundreds of homes a year. Three or four of us each maintained our own thick files for every transaction—30 of them on or near our desks at any one time—covering properties currently in escrow.

The more successful I became, the more properties I sold, creating an endless cycle of growing paperwork. It was burying me—and limiting the growth of my business.

I experimented with all of the transaction management platforms on the market; none of them worked very well. I originally chose

Microsoft SharePoint for my business. It helped—at first—but it wasn't customized to the unique needs and demands of real estate.

So I described my needs to web designers and worked with them to come up with a new application, including features that would meet my requirements as a real estate agent. Finally, my staff and I had a system that worked, and we could also share all of our files at any time day or night on one platform in the cloud.

Although I was paperless as an agent, my broker at the time was not. I convinced him to embrace the platform also, and we created features that let broker and agent work seamlessly in tandem.

At first, my team and I were the exclusive users of the platform. Then I let other top-performing agents from around the country have access to it too. They regularly supplied me with constructive feedback for improving the application, which I turned into new features. When we allowed more brokers to use the system, we made further modifications to the platform to make it more valuable for them as well.

• • •

What became known as SkySlope was growing organically by word of mouth and spreading across the nation. When the platform and I were featured in REALTOR® Magazine, things really took off. So many inquiries came in from agents and brokers that, once again, we were overwhelmed.

As more and more brokerages embraced this platform we did more and more demos, which we then customized for each individual broker's business. Like the agents, brokers also provided constructive input that we adapted for new features.

We joined with the country's top errors and omissions insurance company, which recognizes SkySlope as a great aid in helping agents and brokers conform to legal and regulatory requirements, as well as best practices. The platform's transaction history log provides a digital footprint of all events, including all emails and texts, that take place during a real estate transaction. Each exchange in this digital footprint is date- and time-stamped, and aids agents who strive to be compliant. SkySlope is also a valuable educational tool that can include reminders in brokers' digital checklists for agents to send appropriate emails to their clients and preserve them in the online log.

I realized that SkySlope offered a significant leg up over all the competing transaction management platforms: It can be completely customized to fit the specific needs and wants of every brokerage, and of course, that's particularly beneficial since each one runs its business differently. Recognizing the platform as an important and viable business venture, I relinquished my real estate practice to focus my full-time efforts on SkySlope.

Now more than 40 full-time skilled and committed employees serve subscribers across the U.S. and Canada. Our staff is constantly growing as our business expands. Since our employees fashion SkySlope to meet the special needs of each individual broker, our clientele reflects a rich diversity of companies and the jurisdictions in which they operate throughout the continent. Acknowledging differences is our mantra at SkySlope: Different brokerages. Different states, counties, cities, and markets. No broker we've encountered runs a business precisely like another. So we shape SkySlope to meet each broker's unique situation and systems. That's how SkySlope is different from all of our competitors (even the ones that claim they do what we do).

Our success is built upon:

- Consistently developing the latest breakthrough features, which we issue during regular quarterly releases.
- Offering second-to-none support services that agents and

brokers love because their questions are answered and their problems are resolved 24/7.

- Our expert, intensely trained and experienced activation team that learns a broker's business inside and out, adapts SkySlope to the individual operation, and frequently makes recommendations for improvements—based on our experience with the thousands of brokers with whom we deal all the time—that can allow companies to run more efficiently, thereby saving even more money.

That success is why SkySlope has rapidly spread across the country among big, small, and medium-sized brokers.

• • •

"My business is already paperless," a broker might tell us. That broker will often be convinced otherwise after a brief conversation with us about his or her firm's processes. SkySlope has taken countless brokerages to a new level of understanding about the advantages that come with being truly paperless.

Even the least technologically proficient agents who are most resistant to change have easily learned to use SkySlope. Once they do, these agents never want to go back to the world of paper documents.

Our competitors usually don't have much of a grounding in real estate. They may come from ancillary businesses such as the title insurance industry. Some are tech entrepreneurs anxious to capitalize on the promise offered by real estate technology. Others got into real estate technology after trying to practice real estate themselves without much success.

SkySlope's abiding strength is that it was conceived for agents by a highly successful real estate agent (that's me, of course). It was built with the direct assistance of many of the nation's most successful Realtors® and brokers, and emerged from the daily reality of applying SkySlope to real estate. Hundreds of our clients and advisors continue to advance and sustain SkySlope with the input and suggestions we solicit from them, and often incorporate into the platform. SkySlope is constantly being transformed into the most functional and innovative real estate transaction management application possible.

We provide an innovative product and state-of-the-art customer service by recruiting and retaining the best and the brightest in both the tech world and the world of pragmatic real estate. Working at SkySlope is much more than a typical job; it is a cultural experience that generates high-energy creativity and productivity by people who love coming to work. Our welcoming and stimulating work environment, a casual yet professional attitude that encourages personal growth and collegiality, and a bundle of contemporary amenities and generous benefits all help us to accomplish our additional goal of being a workplace where our people will thrive.

I created SkySlope to liberate myself from the albatross and dreariness of paperwork, so I could concentrate on spending more time with clients and selling homes. Now SkySlope is leading both agents and brokers across North America into the future of real estate.

CHAPTER 1

GOING PAPERLESS

FREEDOM FROM THE BURDEN OF PAPERWORK

"SkySlope frees agents from much of the tedium of paperwork so they can dedicate their time and effort to doing what they do best."

I was born in Sacramento, California, in 1983. My parents were married in Green Bay, Wisconsin, in 1982, then returned to Northern California. My father had grown up in the San Francisco Bay Area, and my parents ultimately settled in the Sacramento region. I was born not long after that. My brother, Riley, followed 13 months later.

Mom says I was an easy kid. She could take me anywhere—to dinner or the movies. I'd sit there and behave, loving to be around people.

We lived in Fair Oaks, a Sacramento suburb off the Highway 50 freeway. My dad worked in a liquor store and my mom taught at Western Career College, a trade school, helping people as they studied to become dental assistants. She's worked there for more than 30 years, and is executive director of the Sacramento campus (it's now called Carrington College), one of the largest in the state.

My dad followed his father and brothers into the concrete construction business, as a foreman on big building projects. He did that work until he passed away in 2006, when I was 25.

It always seemed that my parents' goal was to have us outdoors. The whole family often went camping and on hikes, and we'd travel to rivers where we could skip rocks over the surface.

I LOVED WORKING

When I was 12, my walk to school led to the Rosemont Family Restaurant. They served hash browns, and I loved them. My best friend and I stopped in every day for their hash browns.

By that age, my mom had put me to work doing the household chores: mowing the lawn, folding the clothes, etc. I hated that work. But there was money to be made from my allowance for doing the chores, and I liked that aspect.

My parents conveyed the value of saving money, instead of immediately spending whatever I had on momentary desires. The lesson took hold. That was also okay because I also never liked toys much. When we went to Toys 'R Us, my brother would immediately pick out 10 items he wanted to buy. My mom disliked going there with me because it would take an hour for me to find just one item I liked.

By the time I turned 13, I decided I wanted to go to work at a "real" job. What better place to work than at the Rosemont Family Restaurant where they made the hash browns that I loved. I got a job as a busboy. My hours at work were limited because of the state child labor laws. I had to get a work permit which my parents needed to approve, given my age, but I did it.

I loved working. It made me into who I am today. I learned to think quickly and to think on my feet. I learned how to please others, whether they were my customers or my superiors. I learned to move quickly because I had people—customers and the wait staff—waiting for me to do my job. I learned systems and structures that came with my various job roles: busing and cleaning tables, wiping down seats and putting down all new napkins and silverware and plates precisely as management wanted. There was a system to everything. I loved it—and the discipline that came along with it.

That's also when I learned to love fixing and improving things. There were flaws in the way we would bus tables; the systems were not consistent. They had servers refilling coffee cups. But the bussers were usually the first to see when the coffee cups were empty. So I said, "Why not have the bussers refill the coffee instead?" The manager, who was also the owner of this family-run business, agreed. I worked there through my sophomore year in high school.

Then I started selling firewood. My best friend's family had a cabin up in Georgetown, in the lower Sierra Nevada Mountains on the way to Lake Tahoe. We'd go up there on weekends and my friend's dad put us to work cutting firewood and carting it back for use at their house in Sacramento. A neighbor came by and offered to buy some of the wood. I thought to myself, we could sell this. Awesome.

We became experts at firewood. We had three types: Douglas fir, oak, and pine. We knew oak, a hardwood, would take the longest to burn. That's when I started learning how to sell; I would upsell. "So, you want the Douglas fir," I'd say to a potential customer. "It's the cheapest, but the oak will last longer."

I really learned to sell from watching my dad. I would be with him when he was out wheeling and dealing. He'd talk someone down from a higher price at the flea market. We called him a wheeler-dealer because he always came out on the best side of any deal.

I applied the lessons I learned from my dad to selling people the firewood. We'd pile the wood we cut in the mountains into the truck that belonged to my friend's dad, drive back to Sacramento, unload the wood into a small wagon, and go door to door selling all three varieties. It was fun for a while—although the part about going up into the mountains and chopping the wood we needed was not the fun part. I knew my dad was a very hard worker in his construction job and I didn't want to have to work like that all the rest of my life.

I LEARNED STRUCTURE IN THE CORPORATE WORLD.

The firewood selling, which was seasonal work at best, lasted for about a year.

WHAT CHANGED MY LIFE

I was 16, still a sophomore in high school, when I got my driver's license. I liked my life as a "normal teenager" in high school. I ran track, and I was very good at it. I had long legs and I was quick—so track was for me.

And then I learned, hey, I really wanted this car. It was a black Firebird Trans Am V-8, with a 5.7-liter engine. It looked like the Batmobile.

My mom and dad said if I wanted to have a car I'd have to work for it. So I got a job at Target as a cashier, full-time, with afterschool and weekend hours. I'd stick around to close up after hours—I always had a great work ethic. I worked my butt off, got my dream car and thought I was on top of the world—and I was only 16 then, turning 17.

By the time I was 18, I was promoted to front-end manager, one of the youngest in Target history. It was great. I learned how to manage more than 25 cashiers during the busiest time of the shopping year, which included Black Friday and the holiday season. That's where I really learned structure in the corporate world. I learned how employment worked—and all about the roles of employers and employees, whether in the private or public sectors.

A WHOLE NEW CHAPTER THAT CHANGED MY LIFE.

I learned customer service, including how to deal with both happy and unhappy customers. I learned how to work with and manage people, how to get people to do their jobs, and at the same time how to maintain good morale, which improves productivity. I learned about the incentives people will respond to.

My time at Target was really enjoyable. After graduating from high school I took some time off before college to make more money working full-time at Target. Ultimately I attended community college for a semester or two, and then I transferred to California State University, Sacramento.

The parents of my best friend Clint Kellum were moving all the way up to Eureka, California, near the Oregon border. He didn't want to move. Clint was working at Outback Steak House, telling me how much money he was making off tips as a busser. I thought to myself, I'm working twice as many hours as Clint and he's making more money than me. The competitiveness in me surfaced. I said, I love you, Target, but I'm going to get a new job.

I got a job at Cattlemen's steak house in nearby Folsom. I loved being back in the restaurant industry. It was a little different than when I was 13; I was older and wiser. Also, this was a chain steak house and not a family-owned restaurant. I worked while the place was open between 4 and 10 p.m., the hours that I wasn't taking college classes.

My friend Clint temporarily moved in with me at my parents' house—until we had a thought: Why don't we try buying a house of our own? I wanted to move away from home and strike out on my own. I'd been pretty independent the last several years, and I didn't want to do my folks' household chores any more. I wanted to come home to my own place where there were no limitations.

I was 19, going on 20. The natural desire to move out of the house began a whole new chapter that changed my life.

Clint and I found a Realtor® who also served as our mortgage broker, and this was the person who helped us get the loan. We had saved up $15,000 together, each of us putting up about $8,000, but still needed extra money to cover closing costs. We looked at lots of properties, but we kept getting outbid. We were new at it, and we weren't the most competitive bidders. We finally found a house we really wanted in Citrus Heights, an eastern Sacramento suburb. It was a three-bedroom, two-bath suburban-style single-family detached home. It needed some work, but it was a decent place in a different part of town from where we lived with my parents.

We ended up closing. I had just turned 20. What's ironic is the day we moved in was the same day we each got all four of our wisdom teeth extracted. The dental work happened early in the morning and we moved into our house later that day.

My mother, like any mother, worried about her son. She didn't say I shouldn't buy the house, but she was concerned about the big financial risk I was taking. After all, Clint and I were servers at restaurants. We didn't have predictable, steady incomes. How were we going to make the monthly mortgage payments? That's a big responsibility, my mother said.

I wanted to do the purchase myself, without having to fall back on my parents for support. That was important to me.

So when it came time for Clint and me to buy the house, our parents didn't give us one dime, which is the choice we made together.

We had asked our Realtor® earlier about whether or not we needed a home inspection. Anxious to help us save money, she responded that we didn't. "All it will tell you is the type of dishwasher you have," she said. "You can do that yourself. I know you guys are first-time homebuyers and short on money. Not getting a home inspection will save you $350." That was a lot of money to us—three nights of hard work at the restaurants. She convinced us to dispense with the home inspection.

It's common—and highly advisable—to have a home inspection, but we didn't know that. We didn't ask our parents' opinion because we were intent on being independent. We learned that we'd made a mistake. Humble as I was at the time, it was a question I should have asked at least one of our four parents.

The day we moved in, the hot water heater broke down and needed to be replaced. We called to see if we had a home warranty policy. We hadn't bought that either because our real estate agent was trying to help us save money. She had advised us that a home warranty policy would cost us a lot and nothing would probably go wrong, anyway. Well, it did.

We had to fork over $1,000 to buy a new hot water heater, when we could have had the old one replaced for free if we had spent the $350 on the inspection or the home warranty policy.

DIPPING MY TOES IN REAL ESTATE

At the age of 20, I figured out this Realtor® had not done a very good job. I could see what the real estate agent made on the deal, handling both the loan and purchase. It amounted to about $16,000. I asked myself: If this Realtor® can do a bad job and make $16,000, what could I make if I do a really good job? I knew I could do better, and I mentally put some systems in place to avoid the problems that had befallen Clint and me—and make money in the process.

That's when I decided to leave college. I continued to work at the restaurant afternoons and evenings, but I was spending every morning studying to take my California real estate license exam.

I studied over four or five weeks, took the exam, and passed it. Now I was a Realtor®.

I LOVE TALKING TO PEOPLE WHO ARE MORE SUCCESSFUL THAN ME.

I checked out a number of real estate brokerage firms in the region. One particularly appealed to me because I loved big luxurious homes in California, like the ones they show in Beverly Hills. I discovered a real estate agent, Joe Babajian, who at the time was with one of the state's largest brokers. I wanted to get in touch with him, so I sent him an email and called him on his cell phone, leaving a message asking if I could pick his brain. I'm like a sponge; I love talking to people who are more successful than me. I want to learn from them. I got a call back from Joe Babajian's assistant, saying he had 15 minutes on Thursday to talk with me.

When I got on the phone with him, I told him how I'd like to get into real estate. "What do you like about it?" I asked him. And, "Why is this [the brokerage firm with which he was associated] a place where I could fit in?"

"Kid," he replied, "you can work anywhere you want in real estate. It's you who will make the difference, not the brokerage company. You're the straw that stirs the drink. The brokerage is there to support you, to help you build your career. But your career will not be built by your broker."

"Great," I said, and went to sign up with his brokerage company. They had an office in Folsom, just east of Sacramento. That's where I hung my real estate license for four years.

After I paid a fair amount of money for business cards and fees and other costs, I was really shocked that I was not getting any business. Despite the advice I received from Joe Babajian, my assumption was that real estate was about getting in with a broker, locating yourself in the office, and then people would start calling

I WAS CLOSING ABOUT 100 HOMES A YEAR BY THEN.

you and wanting to buy and sell real estate. I was young and not really educated in the real estate space—they don't teach you about the actual business of real estate when you're preparing for your real estate license exam.

My very first sale was a home in Elk Grove that belonged to my then-girlfriend's father. He was nice enough to let me sell my first house, despite my lack of experience. I got him a great price; it sold for $564,000. It was great money for me. Not bad, I thought.

From there, I sold one or two additional homes that year. I only sold four homes the following year. But I was working full-time and learning that real estate is a tough business.

There was a fellow Realtor® I'd met earlier at the restaurant where I worked, and we had kept in contact. He suggested I check out this guy named Brian Buffini, a prominent coach and trainer in the real estate industry. I said to myself that I should learn from the best. I drove to Carmel, California, and attended what Buffini called his "2-Day Turning Point Retreat™."

It truly was a turning point for me. More than 5,000 people were there, packed into a huge room full of Realtors®. I was the youngest in the room. The retreat was all about how to grow your business. Buffini was animated, encouraging, funny—and he kept me on my toes the whole time. By the end of the two-day retreat, I signed up for a full year of coaching, putting down the $6,000 with his coaching organization, using a credit card. I knew if I didn't pay the full amount, I wouldn't be fully committed to it. And I wanted to make sure I was committed.

Leaving the retreat, I was assigned a coach who called me on a bi-weekly basis. The coach held me accountable to the systems they encouraged, such as best practices and habits. It was simple: "You do this or you're in trouble." They held me answerable for meeting the goals I set for myself.

I saw no progress during the first three months. Zero. However, after three months I started to see some very big results through increased transactions. It was working. My coach always said, "You don't have to be good to start, but you have to start to be good." It was beginning to make sense.

That year I sold 13 homes. Every year after that, I more than tripled my business.

My first two years in real estate were really about dipping my toes into the waters of the profession. I was serious about it, but didn't know how to run my real estate practice like a business. I discovered that most Realtors® don't know how to do that, either.

RAMPING UP MY POTENTIAL

Two things happened to change my prospects as a real estate agent: the first was following the practices from the coaching organization I adopted. The second: my father suddenly passed away from a heart attack.

Even though my brother was already grown up and my mother was successful in her work, I felt like it was up to me to be more responsible for them.

My coach told me to hire an assistant, even though I couldn't afford to pay one. I was spending valuable time doing things that were the least productive—things like paperwork that an assistant should be handling. I knew my best asset was being belly-to-belly with people, generating business and selling real estate. I couldn't do that if I was in the office doing paperwork.

The coach realized that I work best when the pressure is on. Hiring an assistant would put pressure on me to produce. He knew I would make myself go out and drum up the business I needed to create in order to cover the assistant's salary and the income I required. It was the push I needed. I doubled my business over the next 90 days because I was spending more time on my highest priority and my strongest suit, which was being with people. I'm great with people. It didn't take me long to go from hiring one assistant to having three assistants work as part of my team. I was closing about 100 homes a year by then.

After four years in the business, I switched to another major real estate broker. I also decided to change my business model by putting new systems in place that would really ramp up my potential. I learned to put together a team that leveraged my strengths: working with people, and selling properties. By then I had three assistants, two buyers' agents and a listing coordinator—in addition to all the work I was doing. My listing coordinator would set up listing appointments that I went to because what I had to sell was myself: people wanted to do business with me.

After moving from one broker to another, I went from being Number One at the old brokerage firm to being Number Four at the new one. So I approached the Number One Realtor® at the new company and offered to take her out to lunch. "I'd like to pick your brain about why you're so successful," I said.

"Why would I want to let you pick my brain?" she replied.

"Because we can give each other some good ideas," I answered. "We come from different [brokerage] companies so we may have different strategies to share that could benefit us both."

"Why would I do that?" she repeated. "You're my direct competition."

I've always had an open-door attitude when it came to real estate. I remember being a brand new agent, and how hungry I was to learn. Other agents were generous in sharing with me. I felt everyone sharing together is more productive, whether you're in the same market or not. There is so much business to be had out there that it didn't occur to me that our going to lunch and my picking her brain would result in my taking any business away from her.

MY TEAM WAS SELLING 264 HOMES A YEAR BY 2009.

I regularly shared my entire real estate business plan with other people in the business who were interested. My theory is that you give out in slices and it comes back in loaves. This Realtor® at my new brokerage obviously didn't share my perspective.

Another trait of mine is that I'm really competitive. My father was. My mother is. I ran track in high school. I love to win.

Upset—and mad—I went back to my team, slammed the door shut and said, "We have a new goal." I declared, "The new number one goal for us is to do double the business of the number one agent"—the woman who had just rebuffed me. "Whatever we have to do, we will do it. Our goal is to double her numbers—not match them, or do a little bit more than she does. Double them!"

If my team accomplished that goal, every team member plus their spouses would get a fully-paid two-week trip to Maui, on me.

The team did it in nine months. The woman was no longer Number One at our company. I was. I'm not a big bragger. I always say that nothing messes up a good story except numbers. So I didn't say anything—to the former Number One or to anyone else at the brokerage. I let my numbers speak for themselves. My team was selling 264 homes a year by 2009.

A MOUNTAIN OF PAPERWORK

With growing success came another issue: a mountain of paperwork. That year we sold so many homes—and we had to create and keep up-to-date three or four files for each closing. Each

THE SYSTEM WORKED WELL FOR A WHILE, BUT AFTER SOME TIME WE OUTGREW IT.

of my staff members had their own files for every transaction. Each file averaged more than 200 pages. With 264 closings in 2009, that equaled more than 1,000 files that I had to save and store for years because of state Bureau of Real Estate requirements in California.

One Tuesday afternoon at around four o'clock, I got a call from one of my sellers, asking if I could give her an update on where we were over the closing of her property. I scrambled, looking in my files and one of my assistants' files, but I couldn't find information for the update my client was requesting. After some time and trouble, I finally found what I was looking for in the office of one of the other assistants. It turned out that we didn't have matching files. One person would have one particular piece of the transaction no one else had; another staff member had a different piece of the transaction.

At any given time I had a whole wall filled with 30 files, all for properties that were in escrow. My assistants all had the same system with the same volume of files and paperwork. It took me 15 minutes to comb through the files stored up against the walls in three different offices in order to call the client back.

At that moment the realization hit me that I was probably not doing things the way they should be done—using a scalable model. How can you take your business and scale it so it works efficiently? The status quo wasn't scalable. I was limited in the amount of business I could take on, unless I did a better job of being prepared and organized. There didn't seem to be any way to do that with the growing number of properties I was selling. In fact, the more I sold, the more difficult it was to constantly keep all the files updated.

I promised to give all of my sellers a weekly update. But at any given moment I had about 30 clients, and I was having real problems keeping my promise and managing my business at the same time.

I checked out all the online transaction management applications that were available for real estate, but I wasn't satisfied with any of them.

My former girlfriend's father—the one who let me sell my first house—said he might have a solution. "Have you heard of this thing called Microsoft SharePoint?" he asked. "It's a portal through which everyone can access everything having to do with a large company from one single location," he explained.

Once it was set up and operating, Microsoft SharePoint let my team upload all of our documents into one shared file, almost like a drop box. It also allowed us to place notes and add descriptions of property details. And every team member could access the same shared file at any time.

Now, when a client called for an update, I could log in, grab the necessary documents, and supply the requested information quickly.

The system worked well for a while, but after some time we outgrew it. The out-of-the box Microsoft SharePoint software we were using was not customizable for our business in the specialized field of real estate. As we investigated this digital world, we realized that there were other needs we had in real estate that were not being met, either.

SharePoint wasn't meeting my requirements. I wanted to create a customized web-based platform that would.

So I sought out some web developers, described my needs, and agreed on a price for them to help me build something that we called Smith Premier. My sole motivation was to help further my real estate practice as an agent.

It took 90 days for the web developers to develop the new

platform that I implemented. Smith Premier Properties' portal, our web application, wasn't hugely different from Microsoft SharePoint. But it did allow us to meet my needs as a real estate agent. The new platform worked great. It was better than SharePoint—maybe not by much, but the new features we added really made a difference in better serving my requirements in real estate.

Reflecting my open-door attitude towards business, I had begun flying across the nation to meet with other high-performing real estate agents who were as open to sharing as I was. We were not operating in competing markets so that wasn't an issue for anyone. They would ask me what we were doing to manage all of our transactions; they were experiencing many of the same problems as they too generated excessive volumes of paperwork. I told them about the Smith Premier Properties platform I had developed.

"Can we use it too?" they asked.

"Sure, if we can arrange it," I responded. "Let me call my web developers and see if that's possible." I had no background in technology and I had to check to see if it was doable.

My developers said sure, the other agents could be added in, and they could access the platform as users just like my team and I did. Then they could upload all of the transaction files from their practices, the same as I was doing for mine.

As part of our collaborative relationship, my agent colleagues from around the country started calling or emailing me daily with good suggestions for improvements to the platform. Soon, I had 25 agents using the application. Every one of them was among the top 10 percent of Realtors® in the United States. As they utilized the system, they provided me with a lot of feedback on how to make it better.

I agreed with many of the changes they recommended, and we started implementing a lot of them. At that point, after consulting with my accountant, I also realized it was probably a good idea to separate Smith Premier Properties from my real estate operation and create a separate corporation. It was a good business move.

30 DEALS IN 30 DAYS; I CLOSED 34.

That's when we came up with the name SkySlope. Now, it was not our original intention to create a major new business venture. It was more to service my existing real estate business as well as the businesses of the other top agents throughout America who were also using the system.

The thought finally did occur to me that this could be a new business enterprise for me. But I already had a very successful real estate practice. I was making a killing in the real estate market. I was slammed—doing more deals a month than most other agents did in a year. My business coach once handed me a challenge to see if I could close 30 deals in 30 days; I closed 34.

Word about SkySlope had spread among a number of the nation's top real estate producers who were talking it up. A few brokerage companies inquired, wanting to use the system too. I had already started trying that out, with my own broker at the time.

BUILT BY AND FOR AGENTS AND BROKERS

Then, in 2010, I was named one of the top "30 Under 30" by REALTOR® Magazine. Through "30 Under 30," as you would guess, the magazine recognizes the best real estate agents in the country under the age of 30.

There I was, Tyler Smith, then only 27 years old, smiling down from the magazine photo. And I was introduced to every other agent and broker in America as someone who was:

> *. . . up at the crack of dawn. He uses the time for journaling, getting organized, or working out. "This head start is when*

I'm the most creative and accomplish the most," he says. To get in front of REO asset managers and clients, Smith uses a combination of personal notes, newsletters, and "Lunch & Learns." At the lunches, attendees see his smiling mug on the burrito wrappers and pizza boxes, along with the slogan "We deliver." His advice: Ask yourself every day, "How can I make myself stand out and connect with clients?"

The profile emphasized that I "tested a number of transaction management solutions before creating [my] own, SkySlope." The piece also mentioned our web address.

SkySlope was initially built just for me—to help my team and me satisfy our own needs. Then I opened it up to what became about 40 agents and brokers, through a little server powering the application. When REALTOR® Magazine splashed my face—and SkySlope—from coast to coast without any advance warning, we were overwhelmed by the enormous number of agents and brokers who expressed interest in the platform. Our operation had not been built to handle that much interest.

At first, we were unaware of the article, and we panicked. "Why are we getting so many inquiries?" I anxiously asked the developer. "Hardly anyone knows about the website." We had just registered our domain, www.skyslope.com, less than 30 days before. Then we found out about the coverage in the magazine.

REALTOR® Magazine went on to cover SkySlope again in subsequent editions. By that time we had taken steps to handle the substantial increase in inquiries. Lots more of them poured in. In 2010, transaction management—or "going paperless"—was being talked about in real estate, but it wasn't what it is today. Now everyone is going paperless—or trying to; brokers and agents are increasingly making it the norm. In 2010, many people in real estate were asking, "What's paperless? What's this about a cloud?"

After the huge boost in inquiries, I started putting new structures and systems in place, making a conscious decision that SkySlope was a business venture I wanted to pursue.

At that point, the only people working on SkySlope other than me were a few web developers—and they were contract developers, not employees of SkySlope. It wasn't even a business. We had incorporated and owned a domain, but that was only because I saw the necessity of separating it from my real estate practice. In its early phase, SkySlope didn't require a lot of work or time on my part; it pretty much ran itself. There was no support for users, and the fee was extremely modest.

Then I hired our first sales rep. He made calls and set appointments for demonstrations of the platform; I did the demos. Then we would close the accounts. Within a month and a half, we grew from one employee to five. Then we hired an in-house engineer to manage and oversee the expanding group that was contracting with us.

We grew over the next three years to the point where we now have more than 40 full-time employees servicing more than 500 companies that use SkySlope, which demands all of my attention and focus. SkySlope consists of four departments: sales, development, activation, and support. SkySlope is unique because it was built by and for agents and brokers, and that is reflected in how we operate our business.

Our sales department demonstrates our features, products, and systems, usually in response to companies that inquire because they've heard about us.

Our development department is made up of our designers, engineers, and product managers, all of whom are now in-house employees.

Our activation team conducts a complete analysis of each new

WE HAVE A VISION AT SKYSLOPE.

client's pre-SkySlope processes and tailors our platform to match as closely as possible the way the fresh client does business. It oversees the entire process, from the time a subscriber first signs a contract, to the time that the client is ready to officially launch our system.

Our support department supplies skilled technical support and problem-solving for brokers, agents, and their support staff 24/7 via live chat, phone, and email.

In December 2012, our growing operation required the relocation of SkySlope's headquarters, to a new site with much more space. We discovered a historic brick building dating back to the early 1900s, a one-time beer-bottling warehouse, just blocks from the state capitol building in downtown Sacramento. It became SkySlope's home. Our new space, completely renovated, helps us attract—and keep—the best talent in the competitive high-tech world, through a state-of-the-art atmosphere and pleasing environment that motivates team members and sparks creativity.

There are team members at work 24/7, because we're open 24/7. That's also some of what sets us apart from any other company that claims to provide similar services. Agents are always on in real estate. They never really have an off button. While some do try to figure out how to push "off," their first concern is always to get the deal done. We have agents and brokers who contact our support department at 1 a.m. Many agents do a lot of catching up on their paperwork late into the evening. They negotiate and conclude deals via electronic signatures late at night. We also have clients in multiple states and provinces throughout the U.S. and Canada—spread across different time zones. Our clients are always working, so we are always working.

We have a vision at SkySlope: We empower brokers to run their businesses in the most effective way they can, by providing their agents with the best technology in the industry. Having the best technology available also helps the brokers attract—and keep—the best performing agents.

Our applications help brokerages become the offices of the future. SkySlope frees agents from much of the tedium of paperwork so they can dedicate their time and effort to doing what they do best: Being with people and selling properties. That's how I built a successful real estate practice when I was a Realtor®.

CHAPTER
2

GOING PAPERLESS

SKYSLOPE'S UNIQUE ADVANTAGE: CUSTOMIZED TO FIT EACH BROKER'S BUSINESS

"That's why we're different from any other transaction management company out there that says it does what we do."

SkySlope was originally built for me. I used it exclusively when I was a practicing Realtor®. It allowed me and the staff that was part of my real estate practice to collaborate on one platform. (I subsequently gave up that practice to focus all of my efforts full-time on SkySlope.)

Any of us were able to "touch" a file at any given time during the day or evening without having to get up from our laptops or mobile devices. This meant everyone was on the same page, with the same information. It was important because we could move at the pace our customers expected and wanted, and it freed all of us up to spend more time doing what was most important, which was being with our clients.

That was the obvious advantage of going paperless. If I had to waste less of my time—and my staff's time—handling paperwork and the myriad details that go into a transaction, there was more time to spend with clients, prospecting and attracting more business. It worked out perfectly for my team and me, letting us move at a swifter clip and allowing us to update our clients in a timelier manner through the many milestones that constitute any real estate transaction.

Another huge benefit was we didn't have to store four files for each property we were handling. Before going paperless, one file for every current property sat on my desk. My assistant had her own file for each property on her desk. My other assistant had her own file—again, one for every property—at her desk. Another copy of each file was stored somewhere else. Everyone kept their files in the way that was easiest and most convenient for them. None of the files were fully complete; some staff members had materials in their copies of the files that I didn't need to keep, and vice versa.

I realized the benefits of going paperless early on, as an agent. The problem was that my broker was not paperless. Even though my staff and I had a file in the cloud that contained all attendant documents for each client, I still had to print everything out and turn it over to my broker in order to get the necessary approvals throughout the process, and to eventually get paid.

CONNECTING THE PLATFORM TO THE BROKERS

Even though my own operation was paperless, I was still inefficient because I was forced to print out reams and reams of documents—tons of paper—to give my broker.

My platform wasn't connected in any way to the broker side of the real estate business at the beginning.

At that point, I said to myself, Why don't I test it out to see if my current broker will go paperless with me? So I went to my broker at the time—his name was Tim Thompson—and said, "Tim, I'd like to sit down and talk with you about what we're using in our own real estate practice and how it can help the brokerage out. We've created the agent side of the platform and I'd like to discuss doing

"WE NEED TO GO PAPERLESS IN THE COMPANY."

the same for the broker side.

"We need to go paperless in the company," I continued. "I'm paperless. I'm a top-performing agent and I think as a broker who wants to recruit—and retain—top talent, you need top tools and technology. If I build out the broker side of this paperless platform, will you guys be a subscriber?"

Tim hemmed and hawed. He's a great guy, but he was hugely concerned about risk management, as he should have been. He was worried about whether what I proposed doing would be allowed by the California Bureau of Real Estate, whether it would be compliant with state requirements, and whether there would be any legal liability. His biggest concern was how I would get documents signed. As a broker, he is required to sign off on every single item of each transaction he reviews.

Hmmm, I thought. In order to get things signed, Tim will still have to print out all of this paper. Then I went out and did some research, discovering that he didn't have to physically sign them all. It seems counterintuitive, but the broker compliance regulations issued by the Real Estate Commissioner in California does not require any form of signature on documents. It does require brokers to "establish a system for monitoring compliance" with "policies, rules, procedures and systems." It does not say a broker is required to sign or initial each document.

I spec'd out what the broker side of the platform would look and feel like, including all the items we were handling in the paper world at my brokerage firm. Each element of the broker's requirements was laid out, beginning with the checklist, which requires real estate agents to supply certain information and documentation in the particular order established by each broker. Then I replicated the checklist and the submission of all those documents in a digital format that perfectly matched what my own broker needed and in the order he needed it.

Each brokerage company has a different checklist with varying requirements to comply with legal provisions in its state. In the beginning, there was only one checklist in my platform because it was what my brokerage was using. Short sales weren't huge at the time. That quickly changed after the housing bubble burst. Soon I knew I had to have two checklists, then three, then four, and then 12. Now, the possible number is unlimited—SkySlope fully customizes, generates and renames the checklist we create for each and every single subscriber so it conforms to the broker's own operation.

Screenshot of a checklist from SkySlope.com.

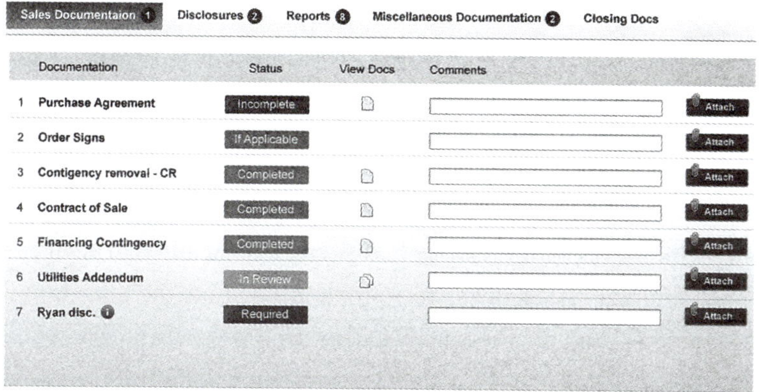

Sales Documentaion 1 | Disclosures 2 | Reports 8 | Miscellaneous Documentation 2 | Closing Docs

	Documentation	Status	View Docs	Comments	
1	Purchase Agreement	Incomplete			Attach
2	Order Signs	If Applicable			Attach
3	Contigency removal - CR	Completed			Attach
4	Contract of Sale	Completed			Attach
5	Financing Contingency	Completed			Attach
6	Utilities Addendum	In Review			Attach
7	Ryan disc.	Required			Attach

BUILDING OUT THE BROKER'S SIDE

I returned to meet with Tim Thompson and showed him what the broker's side of the platform would look like. Tim was still somewhat hesitant. I learned fairly early that brokers like change just about as much as agents do. I also learned they have many valid concerns about legality, liability, and security. I didn't invent

MY NEXT GOAL WAS BUILDING UP THIS PLATFORM I CREATED.

the concept of going paperless. Real estate transaction management was nothing new for brokerages. There were a number of competing companies out there when I spent thousands of dollars looking for and trying other paperless applications. But they never met my needs, which is why I built my own platform.

After patiently going through all of this with my broker, Tim finally agreed to launch a test run of the platform with ten of his agents. It took 45 to 60 days to completely transition from paper to paperless, because it took about 40 days to close escrow on a typical transaction. The platform was a success.

From there we built it out, adding more features based on what the broker needed. Then all the agents at my brokerage firm went paperless, 100 of them at the time. It was a big success.

My broker was in California, where litigation is a bigger problem for agents and brokers than in any other state because—well, it's California. It has the most lawsuits. You get sued for anything. It's crazy.

I had studied the California Bureau of Real Estate rules and regulations. I carefully read numerous cases of lawsuits that occurred in California. What were the problems behind the litigation I examined? Why did the lawsuits arise? How were they disposed of or resolved? I talked with insurance companies that issue errors and omissions policies. What were the most common cases they came across? Why did they come about? All of this research concentrated on identifying the big problems that brokerage firms experience and how a paperless platform could help protect them from litigation or regulatory liability. I used this research to entirely revamp the entire broker side of the platform.

For example, I included a transaction history log. It's a digital footprint of everything that happens in the transaction, covering every checkpoint, every email or text exchange, and every document. The log is date- and time-stamped so it is fully capable of holding up in court or during a regulatory inquiry, if that becomes necessary. It can't be altered or modified. The log won't save you from bad practices in a courtroom. But what's nice is that it paints a picture so anyone can see exactly what the agent was doing at any given time throughout the transaction. It is so much more detailed and verifiable than trying to recall details from memory or documenting it on paper.

I thought then that if I could just get a few other brokers to use this system in California, that would be great. I'd be happy. This still wasn't a business model for me. I was doing great at selling homes, building a successful real estate practice and making a lot of money. I was selling more than $30 million in volume a year. That was huge, for any agent.

So my next goal was building up this platform I created. I knew other brokerage companies, and I decided to let some of them play with the platform and see what it was like. I didn't have a pricing structure in place yet. I wasn't even charging my own broker for the system I designed and implemented for him—and he had acknowledged what a great benefit it was to his business, and he required all of his agents to adopt it.

I started to do some very basic online marketing, turning to Pay Per Click and SEO, which is online advertising. We began organically growing on Google to the point where we held the top ranking for the key words "transaction management software."

Then the calls started coming in. (At the time my cell phone was listed as the contact number.) A broker would call me. "I'd like to take a look at your software," he'd say.

"Sure, I'll do a demo," I'd reply.

We bought some basic screen-share software so the broker and I could be on the same screen at the same time even though we were at different locations, in different cities and sometimes in different states. I'd perform the demo and the broker would sign up on the spot.

That's when I knew there might be a business to develop here. What I also learned was this particular broker ran a company that was very different from the brokerage where I was then working as an agent. Therefore, I would need to modify the platform to fit the needs of this new broker.

Because I had learned that every broker is different, each time another broker signed on, I had to modify SkySlope to fit the needs of that particular business operation. I'd have my platform developers make the appropriate changes. Word of mouth spread about the great job we were doing, and we continued to grow.

Then REALTOR® Magazine covered us—twice: once when I made the "30 Under 30" list in 2010—recognizing the best 30 real estate professionals under the age of 30—and then in an article entitled "Eight Ways to Run Your Office Remotely" in 2011.

It was a big deal for SkySlope to be mentioned in a prestigious national real estate publication. We started receiving many more inquiries. More and more people were filling out our online contact form requesting demos, and sending them to us. Most of the time we performed demos with the aid of screen sharing.

Nevertheless, I was still primarily focusing on my real estate practice. When you are selling as much as $30 million a year—hundreds of deals annually—you're very busy. My practice took up most of my time and that of my staff. But according to the National Association of Realtors® in 2010, the average Realtor® was selling just five homes a year.

My assistant at the time, Jennifer Fernandez, said, "I think you got something here with SkySlope. This is a great tool." And she used it all day long; Jennifer could authoritatively speak about the platform because she was right in the middle of it. I was getting the very same advice from my own business coach.

THAT'S WHEN I KNEW THERE MIGHT BE A BUSINESS TO DEVELOP HERE.

At that point, I decided that if I was going to take this new business seriously, I had to hire my first sales representative for SkySlope. He became the platform's first employee.

Meanwhile, a lot of demo requests were coming in. There were also a lot of follow-up calls that weren't being made because I was so busy with my real estate practice. I learned that when I did the demos, I was particularly good at them because I was in real estate too; when I talked with the brokers who were inquiring, we related well. They quickly understood what SkySlope could mean to them because we spoke the same language—the language of real estate.

My new sales rep also practiced performing demos. But I realized he didn't know real estate like I did; he didn't understand brokers and agents and the real estate community the way I did. The decision was easy: I'd do the demos and my sales rep would schedule them for me. That's what we started doing. I delegated a lot of tasks from my real estate practice to my assistant, who was very capable, so I could concentrate more of my time on SkySlope.

The more demos I performed, the more people wanted to sign up. There was a big rush to get many things in place such as obtaining a business license, opening up credit card merchant accounts and new bank accounts, and putting accounting systems in place. A great deal of this was new to me, because I had just been into real estate, which is what I had eaten, breathed and loved for a number of years.

BEEFING UP SKYSLOPE TO MEET BROKERS' NEEDS

I was doing more and more demos, and more and more people

THIS PROMPTED ME TO BEEF UP MY PLATFORM.

liked the platform. Just as importantly, they were providing me with a lot of good, constructive suggestions for improvement, such as this recommendation: "It'd be really cool if you had different roles, permissions and workflows in the system, like separate ones for brokers, agents, assistants and transaction coordinators."

Then we partnered with the Number One errors and omissions insurance firm in the nation because they saw us as a very compliant system when it came to accommodating all the legal, regulatory and good practice requirements.

Most of the firms we were dealing with at the time were small- to mid-sized brokerage firms. Then I did a demo for a 450-agent company in Arizona, and that broker signed up. However, during our over-the-phone session, I discovered that my platform didn't have everything the new client needed.

The broker-owner of this firm was already using a transaction management application provided free of charge by the local board of Realtors®. But she wasn't satisfied with it and loved what SkySlope could offer. Still, she asked about features we didn't yet have.

Some of the things that SkySlope lacked were different roles and permissions in the platform, and this broker also wanted file sharing—some key items I hadn't previously considered. Also, we didn't have a customer service operation in place. I realized that if this broker had a problem, she was going to call me directly on my cell phone. I already knew from my own experience in the industry that brokers and agents want things done quickly and they need answers at the moment they're asking for them—not later.

This prompted me to beef up my platform to meet her demands. When she signed up I knew my new client had one of the offices of the top 10 producing broker franchises in the state of Arizona; the company had 10 offices and I had signed one of them. If I could do well with her, I figured the other nine offices would sign up too.

That's when I hired our first customer support representative. I put practices and procedures in place. I started setting up a support portal, live online chat, and an 800 number that people could call for assistance. It was a relief not having to take all those calls on my mobile phone anymore.

The woman at the Arizona brokerage franchise office was happy. SkySlope continued growing at a fast pace. The live chat feature on our website was working. A competitor of the Arizona brokerage company came onto our website and asked about our pricing, using the live chat feature. This next brokerage company, with 1,100 agents, signed up too. Because of the advantages SkySlope provides, that company has even more agents and continues to grow even bigger.

'SkySlope is… a big advantage in attracting and retaining high-performing agents'

By Dale Milton, Broker/Owner, *DPR Realty*

I'd been searching for several years for a transaction management program. After looking at three other products, I took a more comprehensive look at what SkySlope had to offer. I wanted a program that would fit our company's needs as well as be simple to use. Agents are very diverse both in their age and knowledge. So I sought a platform anybody could operate to deliver the required information to the company.

I spent a couple of days, along with some of my staff, training in the use of one transaction management system. After two days, I came back to the office and concluded there was no way our staff could use that platform and that it was very agent-unfriendly. It was so cumbersome that trying to put our then-1,100 agents on that system would have been a total nightmare.

Aside from its simplicity of use, one of the leading factors in choosing SkySlope was that an actual real estate agent created it, someone from within our industry. So SkySlope was developed from direct experience with agents' daily need to make more efficient use of their time.

Another instrumental factor was SkySlope's customization of its platform to the particular needs of our company. When I met with Tyler, each time I told him what one of my needs was, he answered, "We can do that." I was blown away. And SkySlope performed everything they said they would complete, without any problems.

During the activation interview process, they asked us many questions about our current processes, about how we do things, about how the agents get their paperwork to us, and about what our staff does with it. SkySlope inquired as to what we saw the platform doing for us and what expectations we had. From there they were able to customize SkySlope to do it.

We were a 100 percent paper company prior to signing on to SkySlope. That required agents to give us hard copies of anything and everything they did. We had a staff of six people who were processing all of that paperwork. After implementing SkySlope we have two people processing through SkySlope instead of six. We were able to move the extra staff over to marketing and recruiting to improve the company's overall visibility in the market.

My staff absolutely loves SkySlope, which is a positive because when the staff are happy, everyone is happy. The staff loves to be able to communicate with agents instantly and (usually) get quick responses back.

We not only significantly reduced our staff hours processing paperwork, but we also reduced our office supply expenses—from having to make hard copies of file after file. We reduced our office supply costs alone by $2,000 a month.

SkySlope has been very advantageous in the area of compliance. Our staff used to get backed up two or three days in processing. Now they are never backed up. Agents get an immediate response, whether paperwork is approved, or whether it's rejected for whatever reason.

SKYSLOPE IS DEFINITELY A BIG ADVANTAGE IN ATTRACTING AND RETAINING HIGH-PERFORMING AGENTS.

The agents know right away where they're deficient. All they need to do is make that correction and reload the file through SkySlope so we can see it. It saves agents a lot of time. It makes for much quicker responses from us to the agents and much quicker responses from the agents to us.

In a lot of cases, SkySlope helps get people their commission checks more quickly. We require files be 100 percent complete prior to issuing checks. Because agents can go online and review their file, they can maintain it and keep it up to date throughout the transaction. Because it's electronic, we can audit files typically within minutes of them being submitted to us. So we see a substantially higher percentage of completed files at the close of escrow and the agents get their checks much sooner.

The state of Arizona requires us to keep transaction files for five years. We have a central warehouse where there are stockpiles of old files. We've been on SkySlope for two years now. That stockpile of files in the warehouse is being steadily reduced. We will completely eliminate the need for all of that space in three years because the files will be available on servers, making for much easier access. State auditors will have quick and simple access to them electronically instead of us having to locate and pull out hard copies from the warehouse.

SkySlope is definitely a big advantage in attracting and retaining high-performing agents. We cite SkySlope in all of our recruiting interviews with prospective agents. We talk about how SkySlope is our transaction management system, how easy it is to use and maintain, and how agents have access to their files 24/7, 365 days a year. Agents really respond to it; they love SkySlope.

They are also starting to recognize it. When we first went with SkySlope it was not a prominently established firm in Arizona. Now, as everyone is hearing what an outstanding product it is, SkySlope is expanding further in Arizona. We talk about the benefits of SkySlope with other brokerage companies. If agents for the buyer and seller are both on SkySlope, it makes transactions effortless; everyone understands the system and what's going on. They can get each other's documents much more efficiently.

CUSTOMIZING SKYSLOPE FOR EACH INDIVIDUAL BROKER

At this point the realization struck—we could offer a vital advantage just about all of our competitors lacked: SkySlope is fully customized to the way any individual brokerage is run. SkySlope does not revolutionize or change the way brokers do business. We mold our platform to their current processes.

Signing up that 1,100-agent brokerage opened the door for us. We were then a small little company with only two full-time employees (not including me). Finally, I clearly saw the light shining brightly at the end of the tunnel and figured out that SkySlope was a viable business that could really succeed. I was convinced.

My big aha! moment had arrived. Making money was never the initial intention. What I knew SkySlope could do was really help brokerages across the nation. It definitely helped the first broker who used it. It helped every broker who subsequently signed up for it. It helped on many levels, not just by reducing paper consumption and saving unnecessary costs. It freed brokers and their agents from the onus of paperwork. Also, what broker or agent wouldn't want to be part of a techie firm?

The real estate industry is moving towards new technology—

and mobility—at a fast pace. So who wants to be stuck doing paperwork—with actual paper? Not any ambitious agent.

THE REAL ESTATE INDUSTRY IS MOVING TOWARDS NEW TECHNOLOGY.

Today, as the CEO of SkySlope, my time is better served by focusing on things other than doing demos. But I did love doing demos back in the day. I'd listen to the broker explain his or her processes and needs. I'd respond by explaining what our platform would do. I even pointed out loopholes and gaps in the broker's processes, and showed how they could be closed or filled in so the brokerage would run better.

Dale Milton, whose then-1,100-agent brokerage in Arizona, DPR Realty, is the one I mentioned that signed up with SkySlope, didn't fully understand the effects—what the platform did for his company. He knew it saved him money and that the firm was happy with us. But Dale and his people didn't truly know exactly why it was such a success for them.

I was out at DPR Realty in Arizona overseeing the SkySlope training of its agents and staff. About eight months later I traveled there again to see how they were doing.

They walked me through the entire office, taking me around the operations we had initially spoken about. They walked me into a large closet-like room, now empty. "This is where we used to store our current files for the year," I was told. "We had a whole warehouse where we stored our old files," they added.

Before SkySlope, they had six administrative staff in the office whose jobs were auditing files and handling all the paperwork, not counting Sharon, the wife of Dale Milton who ran the day-to-day affairs of the office. With SkySlope they were able to rearrange their staff. Now they only need two people to audit and they took their other staff resources and used them for recruiting, which helped increase the firm's agent population by 15 percent. In addition, the company noticed substantial monthly savings on office supplies.

The 15 percent increase in the number of agents working with the broker was on top of the 1,100 DPR Realty already had. Was SkySlope solely responsible for all this growth? No. But SkySlope helped DPR Realty become an effective paperless company and it continues to help DPR attract the kind of high-performing agents the brokerage always sought to recruit.

• • •

When one of my sales reps did a demo for Mike Zagaris, head of PMZ, one of the top brokerages in California's vast Central Valley, Mike instantly saw what we could do for his company; he said he loved the platform and the system. "But I want your CEO to come down here to meet with us," he said.

'SkySlope is the Apple of paperless platforms'

By Mike Zagaris, President/CEO, *PMZ Real Estate*

We had seen the need to transition PMZ into paperless organization for three years already. We investigated six or eight major paperless platforms associated with big national companies, and we found every single platform deficient in one way or another. Most of them were too difficult for our people to use, and we feared the agents and transaction coordinators would not embrace the paperless solution we were going to offer.

Of course, each platform we examined was trying to get one up on the competition. Ultimately, what they all failed to understand was that just because a platform had more features, that didn't mean it was a better platform. Adding more features may seem like a good idea and maybe it is, in some industries. In the real estate industry where brokers are managing agents who are independent contractors, having a platform with 10 great bells and whistles—with lights going on and off and making it look cool and hip—translates to sensory overload.

All the systems we looked at were missing the most important element, which is to have a very simple, streamlined and intuitive system that agents, brokers, and support staff can use easily. It's all about adoption, you see. You can have a great system, but if only your tech-savvy agents adopt it, it's a failure. Most of the other platforms out there can be used by the 5 percent of agents who are technologically advanced. But the average age of a Realtor® today is 57. Even more importantly, most sales volume is skewed towards those who are 57 years or older. They are the ones who have been in the business the longest and have built up a following over time. Most of those agents won't end up using any of the fancy features.

When we at PMZ try to roll out a new tool for our agents, we always make sure it's very simple and straightforward. Eventually, that was the problem with all of these other platforms we considered. While some had great features in and of themselves, when taken altogether, they were all too cumbersome for agents and brokers to use on a daily basis.

So we decided to build our own transaction management platform using our own in-house technical talent.

Literally within a week of making that decision, we received a phone call from a SkySlope sales rep offering their services. Greg Smith, our IT department head, asked for a demo at my request. At first, our IT guy was reluctant to waste his time looking at yet another platform. And it's important to remember that Greg had a vested interest in telling me this new platform was also inadequate, because he was going to be the one to develop our in-house system and probably spend a year doing it. But Greg took a look at SkySlope.

He returned to me after the demo and said, "Mike, they have it all figured out. It's exactly what we were planning on building. These guys have done everything right. They've gone down the path we would have taken, only far better than we would ever have done it."

SkySlope is the Apple of paperless platforms. It is simple, intuitive and very technical, but not intimidating. The reason SkySlope works is because Tyler Smith designed it and he comes from within our industry and has an intimate understanding of our needs.

I told my IT guy, "Great, but tell the [SkySlope] sales rep that I want his CEO, Tyler Smith, who designed the platform, to come down here and do a demo himself." SkySlope is based in Sacramento, so Tyler didn't have far to travel to Modesto, where PMZ is headquartered.

A week later, Tyler showed up and performed the demo. He was articulate and precise. In one presentation he was able to convince our entire executive team to go with SkySlope. There was a feeling of relief that we weren't going to have to develop this entire system from scratch. We were thrilled about how cost-effective it was. We were excited to be entering the digital world in this way, and excited at the prospects of continuing moving our brokerage firm forward on a progressive path. Our obligation as a broker is to stay on the cutting edge for our agents.

That's also how we attract and keep top agents. We knew SkySlope would be an effective additional recruiting tool.

SkySlope's activation process was effective because they asked a lot of questions. They came in with direct and pointed questions about how our business works, and why we do what we do—from why our review process is structured the way it is, to why we have commission checks go to individual PMZ offices instead of coming to one office. They created a workflow model for us.

The activation reps at SkySlope have the advantage of working with hundreds and hundreds of brokers from across the country.

They see how all of them work effectively and not so effectively, and pass along their insights to the rest of us. After the activation process, PMZ streamlined all of our processes. The savings from that streamlining has more than made up for what SkySlope costs us on a monthly basis.

WE WERE EXCITED TO BE ENTERING THE DIGITAL WORLD IN THIS WAY.

While SkySlope worked on customizing its platform to our needs, our executive team shared with our agents all the positive advantages the platform would bring to their individual real estate practices. Each week we sent out videos explaining how excited and eager we were to unveil this platform in the weeks to come, how it would allow the agents to be able to access their files at any time on any given day or night, how it would free them from paperwork so they could spend more time with clients and drumming up new business, and how it would allow them to be paid more quickly.

We played a very proactive role in the rollout of SkySlope. Our goal was never to say the new system was mandatory; we never used that word. We expected that the agents would want it and ask for it. The most important thing to remember about managing independent contractors is that they really are very independent and very individualistic. Announcing that SkySlope would be mandatory and that they could no longer use paper files would not be a good way to go.

By the time SkySlope was rolled out, we had built up the hype and articulated the power of the platform, so immediately—in the first month—we had a 75 percent voluntary adoption rate among our agents. The remaining 25 percent came on board in the second month. Sixty days after the rollout of the platform, PMZ was entirely paperless—and no longer accepting any paper files.

We were immediately able to get rid of one of our closing department staff members because we could spread the work out

SIXTY DAYS AFTER THE ROLLOUT OF THE PLATFORM, PMZ WAS ENTIRELY PAPERLESS.

better. Before, we had all these different offices, each with front office staff. When a transaction file came into the office, only one set of eyes could look at it. With SkySlope, we divvied up the work among any reviewers who had time to look at it in the cloud, no matter where those people were located. You could be in our San Francisco Bay Area office and review files from our Modesto office in the Central Valley if you had an extra hour in your day.

We eliminated the courier costs of shuffling bulky files from office to office. And we got rid of our warehouse, which we no longer needed for file storage, after converting all of our paper records into digital ones. Paper and office supply expenses were also almost eliminated.

Before SkySlope, the manager in each office would initially review the file and give it back to the agent who managed it for the rest of the transaction. When the transaction was finished, the agent would fold all the disclosures and other pertinent documents into the file, which would be closed and sent to the closing department at our corporate office, where it would be reviewed. Files are almost always missing a signature or an initial somewhere, no matter how diligent the agent is. With files often five inches thick, something will be left out. When we discovered what that was, we would have to alert that agent that a file was missing something on page 68, for example. The agent would have to get in touch with the buyer or seller to get it initialed. Even if the client who was doing the initialing was totally knowledgeable and in agreement, an "incomplete" file was still not compliant with state laws or regulations.

If something is missing now, SkySlope red-flags the item and immediately sends a message from the closing department to the agent. The great thing about SkySlope is that you're uploading documents as you go along during the transaction. When the agent's contract is signed, it is entered into the system and gets reviewed. A few days later the disclosures are signed and uploaded. Two weeks before the close of escrow, agent and broker can know everything is in compliance so when the transaction closes, the agent gets paid.

SAVING MONEY AND STAYING COMPLIANT

Emails are a huge thing in the modern age. So are text messages. You're the broker. How do you see email or text messages constantly flowing back and forth between your agents and their clients? SkySlope keeps them and makes them available to you at any time, no matter where you are. No other transaction management company does that. We save and maintain authorized access to email and text exchanges—all of them.

When the economy was hurting during the Great Recession, financing for home purchases dried up and the housing market tanked. Americans were buying many fewer houses. America went from having approximately 1.6 million Realtors® to about 1 million Realtors®. State departments regulate Realtors®—and impose dues, fees, and fines.

When the real estate market was hot and countless transactions were flying through the system, state regulators could barely keep up with the volume of activity. When things dramatically slowed down with the recession, the regulators reexamined what they had been doing, and as a result, demanded new requirements and reports.

There were fewer practicing agents and less competition. As a real estate agent, I noticed a marked increase in audits in the industry. State regulators at that time also wanted to do a better job of protecting the public and making sure everyone in the industry was in compliance with the rules, which is a good thing.

One of those rules requires brokers to keep records of every one of their real estate transactions for between three and nine years, depending on the state. Nationally, the average size of a transaction file is 93 pages, based on SkySlope's extensive data. The average in California, with its greater regulation, is more than 200 pages; if a homeowners association is involved there can be another 300 pages of rules, regulations, and bylaws that by law must be preserved in the transaction file.

All of those pages need to be kept in a file. The pages need to be hole-punched. They require paper clips. Labels are needed to identify various subjects, including listings, inspection reports, contracts, correspondence, and disclosures.

You, the broker, need to be able to find the file and ensure it's not been damaged or destroyed. That means sometimes storing huge volumes of paper files in warehouses that brokers either own or lease.

What did you think happened to real estate brokerage companies' stored transaction files when Hurricane Katrina devastated whole sections of New Orleans?

Elsewhere, the office building of one SkySlope's client burned to the ground. If this brokerage had been relying upon paper files, it would have been gravely out of compliance. With everything else that broker had to worry about after the fire, legal liability was not a concern because all of the firm's transaction records were safely preserved and stored in SkySlope's cloud.

After brokers have stored and maintained their paper records for the prescribed three to nine years, at the beginning of the fourth or tenth year, they have to laboriously shred all of these voluminous records in order to protect their clients' confidential information. That costs more money too.

We have found that paper-office brokerages that switch to SkySlope save, on average, more than 25 percent of total annual expenses.

TIME IS A LUXURY THAT GOOD AGENTS DON'T HAVE.

• • •

I learned as a former practicing real estate agent that if you ever have to go to court or be on the receiving end of regulators' investigations, it all comes down to what you have in writing to prove your case. To this day, too many agents and brokers confront a big gap when it comes to demonstrating compliance in real estate.

There is usually a lot of talk going on between agents and their clients, and not a lot of documentation. Too often—actually about 80 percent of the time—if a dispute ends up in a court proceeding or a state department of real estate investigation, it's all about "he said" or "she said." There's usually not enough paper documentation to substantiate the agent's or broker's side of the story, or to cover their legal liability.

A solution, when using the paper system from the old real estate industry, went like this: Agents could print out a copy of all the emails to the buyer or seller and place them in the application file so they are available in case of a disagreement. Normally, agents wouldn't keep such records in real time. To generate those files, agents, at the end of transactions, would have to arduously sift through all their emails from the past months, locate those relating to a particular buyer or seller, select them, print them out and bring them to the broker's office so they could be placed in the proper file. This would take a great deal of time. Time is a luxury that good agents don't have a lot of. Simply, agents just aren't going to do it.

The solution in SkySlope's system is the transaction history log, a digital footprint of everything that happens in the real estate transaction. SkySlope records exactly when emails or texts are sent as part of this digital footprint, date- and time-stamped so they will pass muster in any judicial or regulatory proceeding. Our subscriber base is utilizing this proven method for capturing all communications between agents and clients now.

This is why Pearl Insurance®, one of the largest errors and omissions insurance providers in the nation, is working with us. Pearl took a look at SkySlope's platform and concluded, "You are pretty compliant," and now offers discounts on premiums for SkySlope subscribers. It's similar to "good driver discounts"—breaks on car insurance premiums—that many auto insurers offer their motorist clients who have clean driving records.

SkySlope can provide this legal security, but of course agents still need to make sure to send their clients the emails. We save and preserve them for the agents who do. For agents who don't yet practice this important habit, SkySlope serves as an educational tool. It can be incorporated into the checklist brokers require their agents to abide by. Furthermore, SkySlope sends agents reminders to forward their email correspondence into the log to be preserved.

DIFFERENCES BETWEEN SKYSLOPE AND ITS COMPETITORS

Subscribers throughout the U.S. and Canada use SkySlope. Our staff customizes the platform to meet every broker's needs, and there is a diverse array of requests, given the diversity of companies and jurisdictions, each with its own special demands and requirements.

Six out of the top 10 franchise brokerages in California exclusively use SkySlope. We have a 35 percent market share in California among brokerage companies. Nationwide, we handle everything from luxury boutique brokerages such as Hilton & Hyland, a high-end 140-agent brokerage in Beverly Hills, all the way up to a large multi-office brokerage that is number one in the state of Pennsylvania on the opposite end of the continent. These broker firms cater to completely different clienteles and are governed by totally distinct state laws and regulations. Our platform is specifically tailored for each one of them.

EVERY BROKER IS DIFFERENT.

That work is accomplished for SkySlope through a workforce that now boasts more than 40 skilled and dedicated full-time employees.

SkySlope issues a release every quarter of new breakthrough features based on feedback we receive from our users. We constantly and consistently build the platform so it is 100 percent customizable for every broker, molded exactly to their wants and needs.

I can't say it often enough: Every broker is different. Each company is different. Every state, county, city, and market is different. We've yet to come across any broker who operates in exactly the same way as anyone else. That's why we're different from any other transaction management company out there that says it does what we do.

Much of our success is centered on our activation team. It strives to quickly understand a new subscriber's business and then apply our application to what that broker is already doing. If a broker is operating the business perfectly, that's great. We adjust to it. But if we can also offer advice and tips on adopting efficiencies we observe from working with hundreds of top brokers all across the country, then we can help make the broker's business even better.

Once a brokerage company signs with SkySlope, it is immediately assigned to an appropriate activation rep specializing in firms of that size.

All of SkySlope's employees, and especially our activation reps, go through an intensive three-to-four-month real estate training course. They begin with basic Real Estate 101, covering the ins and outs of the business, material that every agent and broker does or should know.

100 PERCENT CUSTOMIZABLE FOR EVERY BROKER.

Activation team reps undergo an additional 30-day crash course, where they are assigned to several real-life brokerages. They learn how things worked under the pre-paperless regime and what going paperless does for people in the industry today. They accompany agents and brokers by going out into the field to experience the actual lives of real estate professionals. Our activation reps can't be knowledgeable and offer sound advice unless they themselves have thoroughly experienced the day-to-day reality of how agents operate, from watching agents write up initial offers to closing on properties, plus everything in between.

That's the difference between SkySlope and its competitors. Our people eat, breathe and sleep real estate. They receive daily Google alerts on anything and everything having to do with the industry.

As a former practicing real estate agent, I created a 32-point checklist for myself to help me get more business. I adhered to it religiously. I took the same principle and applied it to what our activation department does in helping new subscribers launch SkySlope.

The substantive work begins when the activation rep conducts a process call with the new subscriber. It usually takes about an hour, depending on the company's size. The rep takes extensive notes during the conversation. And the rep doesn't hang up until he or she comprehends the broker's entire business and the specifics of how it operates inside and out.

After conscientiously investigating what the broker does from A to Z, we design our platform to meet that brokerage's needs. One broker will have a single staff person who reviews all the files of agents in the office during the transaction process. Some firms have four reviewers. So we fashion SkySlope to include certain workflows that are applied by each relevant support staff person at each step in the process, tailored to when in the company's process he or she needs to use them. Everyone maintains the same roles they've always performed, only now they're geared up to work in the digital world of SkySlope.

Following are samplings of how major brokers from around the country, some of whom had experiences with other paperless systems, evaluate SkySlope.

'SkySlope serves us better'

By Stacy Hall, Broker/Partner, *Keller Williams*

I had used a competing transaction management platform for a couple of years before turning to SkySlope. SkySlope serves us better. Plus, the responsiveness of its customer service is far above our expectations.

SkySlope worked with us to fully customize our platform to meet all of my needs and expectations. What works is the fact SkySlope has hands-on control over all of its platform programmers; SkySlope directly employs all of them. That's intriguing because I know as a business owner myself that when you have to rely on other people you don't know how long the task will take to get done. You don't have to wait around for someone else to respond with SkySlope.

The back-end administrative feature allows us to personally customize checklists when needed without having to rely on SkySlope to make the changes or additions. The fact that we can customize or modify our requirements at any time ourselves—that's huge. The SkySlope system also allows us the capability to add new agents when they join our company and remove them when they leave us so they can no longer have access to the system.

I thought we would have more of an issue when we converted to SkySlope. The first paperless platform we used required a two-week conversion. When we decided to convert to SkySlope the conversion took two days. I had very little if any negative feedback from agents. There was some frustration if an agent had missed part of the training from SkySlope. It was completely erased once we pointed the agent to SkySlope's 24/7 online chat so he or she could be walked through everything.

The 24/7 support services at SkySlope relieve approximately two hours a day of interruptions of my auditing staff from agents asking questions. Before SkySlope, I had a designated person at each of my four offices responding to questions. Now my auditing staff no longer deals with those questions—SkySlope's support department handles them directly.

The ease of the SkySlope system allowed us to consolidate the number of people needed to audit our transaction load. Before I had to have an auditor sitting at each site. Since switching all of my offices to SkySlope I have been able to centralize into one main office, allowing for better supervision of the auditing process. With the task of auditing files taken off of those staff members, their time is now better spent doing other tasks—and that makes for a more efficient operation.

We had our first outside audit several years ago, which brought much more awareness to our staff and agents of the importance of having a complete file. Because of that, compliance was a huge factor in what we were looking for from SkySlope. The platform is very transparent insofar as through SkySlope the agents understand what they must do to be compliant and the platform is so simple that anyone can understand it; it's all color-coded. SkySlope's system forces our agents to stay in compliance with all of their paperwork by holding them accountable for a complete file so that file can be archived and so they can get paid.

Laws and regulations are constantly changing in the state of California. Therefore, we are probably a little overly compliant when it comes to disclosures. We make sure our checklists require the proper disclosure documentation as it relates to specific types of transactions.

With SkySlope, you can also customize your checklist to each specific type of transaction. This allows us to put documentation requirements into the checklist to ensure the agents are aware of the specific disclosure requirements. A short sale or REO requires different types of disclosures than a traditional sales transaction. What's great about SkySlope is that we have the internal capability of creating separate checklists for different types of transactions. SkySlope makes sure agents are aware of the appropriate disclosure requirements and contractual documentation.

'SkySlope understands real estate from a practitioner's outlook'

By J. Scott Leonard, President/CEO, *Guarantee Real Estate, a Berkshire Hathaway Affiliate*

We had a disastrous previous experience with a transaction management system that caused me to be very, very cautious in going back to an online paperless platform. Another broker who is very respected recommended SkySlope.

What impressed me about SkySlope was that it clearly understood real estate transactions from a practitioner's viewpoint. SkySlope was built in a way that caters to the needs and skills of the actual in-field practitioner instead of taking it from the perspective of an analyst or programmer who is trying to understand our industry. SkySlope is based on actual knowledge taken from a user orientation.

Our previous platform was based on the opposite mindset, which is why it wasn't functional or efficient for my people. After two weeks of trying, I pulled out of the whole thing. That's why SkySlope made all the difference.

We were very impressed with its flexibility. SkySlope came in and asked how they should adjust and configure their product to meet our needs. Then they worked with my staff to get it done. We're just one of hundreds of companies that use SkySlope. Each company approaches transactions a little differently. I don't know how SkySlope does it.

Each company basically has a standard set of documents required for any transaction. How we assemble them, float them through the system and set up the controls and procedures are important to us. Even though our specific document checklists are different from those of other companies, SkySlope incorporated our methodology of doing transactions into its product. So when they were first introduced to SkySlope, it was familiar to my agents and staff. The formats they were looking at online were consistent with the processes and practices they had always used—as opposed to a plug-in platform that tells agents and staff, "Here's the system; you reconfigure how you work to meet it." SkySlope conformed to our company's methods of handling transactions.

Since the agent population is diverse both in terms of age and technological capacity, we first beta-tested SkySlope for a few months at two of our offices. It went well. Those offices became champions of SkySlope throughout the company. Full implementation happened over 30 days. There was not a lot of push-back. It's been a year since the first rollout on a limited basis and 10 months since it became a mandatory corporate system tool for all 550 of our agents in our 10 offices.

The 24/7 support services are also an important part of the product. It is fairly unique to be able to reach a live body at any time.

Our people were used to relying on staff or management when they had issues, so they went there first. We've retrained people so they know SkySlope's customer service resources are available. Today, there are very few questions and when they come up, our people go directly to SkySlope.

The efficiencies in SkySlope can increase agents' productivity by reducing the amount of time handling and delivering paperwork between agents, brokers and clients. As people embrace this technology, SkySlope results in more efficient use of agents' time.

'SkySlope's team is top-notch and very professional'

By **Matthew Crumbaugh**, President,
Allison James Estates & Homes

We had built our own file management system prior to switching to SkySlope, but it wasn't what we wanted. SkySlope came highly recommended by one of my agents. It is not a difficult system to use.

We're not a traditional company or a franchise brokerage located in just one area. My agents don't work out of brick-and-mortar offices, necessarily; we don't have a broker in an office with 100 agents. They can't walk in and turn over a contract to my broker. They have to submit their files online; they work virtually, for the most part. I'm essentially running one corporate office that is covering agents in 15 states.

So having a system and technology that was right for my unique business model was very important. Everything had to be able to be easily submitted through SkySlope. When we did the initial activation process with SkySlope we ran into big issues right away because we're not structured like everyone else.

SkySlope took the lead. "Matt, don't worry," they said. "We're going to build a custom platform just for you." Doing that will be pretty pricey, I thought, and offered to pay extra. SkySlope just made it happen—and made sure we had what we needed. That was huge for me. It showed me the type of business SkySlope is.

It wasn't easy. We have 15 different sets of laws, regulations, and documents—a different set for each state. The kicker was how we separate them all out. Everything had to be customized for each of the states. We were also rolling out accounting systems that all had to be integrated hand-in-hand with the 15 states. SkySlope took the bull by the horns and worked hard. We got a really nice system that works.

The functionality of SkySlope—for example, in how documents are approved—makes it an easy system on the agents. It makes compliance easier. The system itself has checks and balances. When our broker doesn't approve a document because, say, it's missing a signature, the system sends out a notice to the agent's iPad or iPhone with a screenshot of the document telling him or her what to do. With today's technology, everyone is using these devices. SkySlope puts the issue directly in front of the agents without them having to log into the system at the computer. It notifies the agents when they're traveling, or doing whatever, that they have to take action.

Then there's the tracking of transactions, with everything date- and time-stamped to provide documentation.

With our previous online system, I had to have IT people on staff to field support questions. SkySlope's support team is there 24/7. At first, I really wondered if they would be there 24/7, but they are—and they are very, very responsive.

My big thing about SkySlope is that it is a model in how to run an organization. SkySlope's team is top-notch and very professional.

'SkySlope adapts its online world to how brokers run their deals'

By **Larry Matos**, President, *Century 21 M&M*

Large brokers throughout the industry are searching for on-line solutions. SkySlope is one company out there along with a list of many others. We checked out many of them. We were with another online platform for several years, but it wasn't working. We talked with a lot of our broker friends about the platforms they were using and why. A lot of them said how easy SkySlope was and the high adoption rate of agents using it.

The biggest reason we switched to SkySlope was its usability and high adoption rate. It's very transparent and easy for agents. It also has important features for transaction coordinators, assistants and broker-managers that fit well with our organization since we have a lot of them. The system really caters to the needs of a traditional company like ours with 29 locations and more than 1,200 agents.

Real estate is very unique to the broker and his offices. When you have a vendor with strict business rules in how the system is to be used, it makes it very hard on our end to get the adoption rate we need. Brokers want flexibility in how they run their businesses. SkySlope offers that.

The customization of SkySlope to our operation was a positive factor in that we got high adoption rates from agents and managers. There was a lot of communication between our team and SkySlope's team. We got to know one another. They are good listeners at SkySlope. We feel comfortable with their system and they understand our needs and how we handle transactions. SkySlope adapts its online world to how brokers run their deals.

SkySlope is the product of a real agent who was in the business for quite a few years and did a lot of transactions. SkySlope knows the expectations of brokers, agents, buyers and sellers. SkySlope has walked in our shoes and understands where brokers and agents come from.

A lot of other transaction management companies are publicly traded or are run by highly technical people who haven't run real estate transactions. They don't understand the day-to-day ins and outs of running a real estate brokerage, and working with buyers, sellers and agents. You truly need that real world experience to understand how a real estate office functions.

We've gained enormous efficiencies from SkySlope. We looked at three questions in searching for an online platform: Is it efficient? Is it cost effective? Is it risk management compliant? SkySlope met all of those needs.

We reduced our paper expenses by 50 percent in the first three weeks after rolling out SkySlope, and that number keeps going down each month. It's the same with paper, toner and equipment costs. Plus, SkySlope is much more effective in reviewing transactions.

SkySlope's DigiSign™ electronic signature feature is time-stamped; you can track when the client signs a document. SkySlope stores all back-and-forth emails. We have checklists we create for all different kinds of transactions; if something is not met on a checklist, we're notified immediately.

We have managers and file reviewers who oversee the managers' work, to make sure we're in compliance during the entire process of the transaction and when it closes. With SkySlope, we know if something's missing and can identify it really quickly.

If I'm a broker out there looking for an online product, I'd definitely investigate more than one or two of them to find the right fit for my business practice. With SkySlope, you get a very qualified and responsive team with support available 24/7. Very few companies have that. If agents have problems, SkySlope is there to respond and walk them through to the solution.

Before SkySlope, we were with the biggest competing online platform. It had no 24/7 support. So the broker or manager at our company had to walk agents through their problems. You need qualified people who understand their own online system to manage it and get a high adoption rate; it has to be the same people who design the system who are there on an ongoing basis 24/7. That's what increases the adoption rate among agents and staff.

Our adoption rate is probably 95 percent. That's very good. It comes down to SkySlope's support and customer service—that's been a pivotal point in getting agents to embrace and use the system. The 24/7 support is where SkySlope has a leg up on all of its competitors.

Brokers are all cut from the same cloth. If we're paying a fee for a service we want to make sure we're utilizing that service. If you pay a fee and agents are not using it, then you're not utilizing the service. Our agents have embraced the SkySlope system.

'SkySlope has a user-friendly interface so it's not scary'

By Glenn "Chip" Gardner, VP of Special Initiatives,
Gardner, Realtors®

We were looking at the landscape of integrated transaction management and digital signature platforms when another tech savvy broker we trusted referred us to SkySlope. A lot of the time people say SkySlope helps them go paperless. Paperless is a good thing and a byproduct of the platform is it helps us be greener and reduce the amount of paper we use. But SkySlope's other function within a real estate company is creating operating and risk management efficiencies.

SkySlope is for the benefit of real estate agents. It empowers agents by providing them with a centralized dashboard where they can be in control all of their transactions. It assists brokers in supporting agents by having everything agents need in a centralized location. So if an issue ever arises, there is easy and immediate access to information for all the parties involved.

One of the biggest things about SkySlope for me is that it makes agents more efficient by putting all their transaction paperwork in one easy to navigate electronic folder so they don't have to have all of these paper files everywhere if they don't want to. Agents can pull anything they need to reference at any time since we are always connected to the Internet.

As part of her plans for a month-long European trip, one of our agents was planning to hire an assistant to sit at her desk in the office in case the need arose to pull anything from her transaction files while she was away. We asked if she had started using SkySlope yet. She had not. After this agent was trained in SkySlope, she realized there was no need to physically locate an assistant in her office because she can simply control all of her ongoing transactions even while outside the country by utilizing SkySlope.

By making our agents more efficient they don't have to spend as much time on paperwork and can instead focus on generating more business.

SkySlope is also an asset when it comes to risk management. When one looks out at the regulatory horizon, most people will agree that the trend is increasing for more regulation and litigation. SkySlope helps better protect the agent and broker by ensuring that all the appropriate documents in the transaction are properly executed and securely stored in case it is ever needed for future reference.

We looked at other systems but at the end of the day decided on SkySlope because a skilled real estate agent designed it for use by other agents. SkySlope follows the KISS principle—Keep It Simple Stupid. Some transaction management systems make things overly complicated and do not include the integrated digital signature component. We wanted a system that keeps it as simple as possible while giving us all the functionality we need. Ninety percent of Excel users only use 5 percent of its functionality. You want a transaction management platform to keep it simple for everybody or you will have agents and brokers who won't utilize the system. That's what SkySlope does; it has a user-friendly interface so it's not scary.

SkySlope's 24/7 support services, which are based on the principles in the book Raving Fans, are also absolutely critical for agents and brokers. It is comforting to know you have someone to reach out to at any time to give you support.

UNIQUE CULTURE YIELDS INNOVATION AND PRODUCTIVITY

Every successful business enterprise and social or political movement establishes its own culture, and SkySlope is no exception.

Central to SkySlope's success is creating the most innovative real estate transaction management product and the best possible customer service. We do that by drawing upon the best and the brightest talent in the tech world. So we view keeping employees satisfied as a vital piece of our platform's culture.

How many people do we know whose lives revolve around looking forward to escaping from the burden of work for the weekend, or taking that annual vacation, or eventually retiring so they don't have to work any longer? One of the best things that can happen in your life is loving the work you do. I want everyone at SkySlope to be smiling and as happy as I am to come to work each day. It's pretty amazing how much more enjoyable work is when everybody around you is glad to be there.

We've worked hard to make SkySlope into a cultural experience that has yielded ever-increasing productivity, next to zero job

I WANT THEM TO LOVE COMING IN TO WORK ON MONDAYS.

turnover, employee contentment that remains extraordinarily high, and a near-perfect 96 percent satisfaction rating among our subscribers. SkySlope's reputation is rapidly spreading across the nation.

We lost our first sales rep because he and his wife moved back to his native North Carolina for family reasons. Another employee returned to Arizona for the same purpose. A third employee left to return to her seaside college town, San Luis Obispo, which she missed. That's it for turnovers at SkySlope.

SkySlope's work force appreciates the casual but professional on-the-job atmosphere, surrounded by a modern office environment sporting brick walls and vibrantly colored rooms. Our company headquarters isn't just aesthetically pleasing; we provide an array of meaningful amenities that make it welcoming and stimulating. Add to that SkySlope's generous employee benefits, including complete health insurance packages, daily catered food, our own rituals where we have fun together, free parking, and an array of other perks, such as a $100-a-month allowance for "wellness." It can cover free gym memberships, scheduled massage appointments, Lake Tahoe ski lift tickets, or green fees at golf courses. This mix of a positive work atmosphere and good employee treatment is rare where we operate. It pays off in what SkySlope is continuously able to offer our subscribers.

We recently equipped everyone at the office with Fitbits, the little devices you wear on your wrist like a watch. They measure every step you take during the day or night, and help mark your progress towards a healthier and more active lifestyle. By hooking the fitness tracker right up to their mobile device, staff can regularly track their levels of activity. One of the ways we reward our employees is based on how active they are. Every day the steps that each person takes are translated into points that the staff earns. For every 100 steps taken, the employee earns one point. Once they hit 500 points, they earn a coin, the currency they use to redeem their rewards with the company. Rewards include gift cards to Starbucks, Amazon, iTunes, and Spotify (an online music store providing access to millions of songs), or favorite restaurants.

Healthier employees are happier employees. That also translates into fewer sick days and higher performance.

People stay with us for a lot of reasons. One is that our management team matches our generous perks and benefits with generosity of praise where it is deserved, honest feedback, and constructive opportunities to learn and improve when people under-perform. Everyone at SkySlope works hard to move up.

Fulfilled employees are more likely to work harder. They give more and go the extra mile for our clients. I want them to love coming in to work on Mondays. I think everyone deserves a job where they can do that.

At SkySlope we have invested much time and effort cultivating a culture that breeds familiarity and geniality among workers. It ranges from the support and communication that occurs between departments, to Potluck Wednesdays, where each department in the company switches off fixing picnic-style lunches for the entire office as well as games during the day. Such undertakings may appear unorthodox for a business, but the results are further demonstrated in the reputation SkySlope enjoys among our consumers.

"It's a great experience due to the fun, laid-back yet hard-working culture—and the amazing people working here," affirms Kais Mustafa, one of SkySlope's own.

• • •

SkySlope headquarters is on a quiet, tree-shaded residential street in downtown Sacramento, just blocks from the ornate state capitol and city hall.

We took over a one-time warehouse and beer brewery bottling plant that is more than 100 years old. The first floor of this historic structure was raised above ground so it would be level with the beds of huge horse-drawn wagons to ease rolling beer barrels through the large brick doorways that are still visible.

I love this building, which is so common among one-time downtown warehouses that boast exposed 100-year-old brick.

Our large gated parking lot empties onto a series of wood stairs that lead to an elaborate redwood deck overlooking a landscaped courtyard. Employees can use the deck's heated Jacuzzi, as well as have their lunch at the deck's picnic tables when they want to eat outdoors. String lights illuminate both exterior and interior spaces.

Once in the main entrance, instead of the traditional reception room with chairs and magazine tables, you are greeted by a foosball table, and beyond it to the left, a room with ping pong and pool tables. Immediately to the right is a pop-up office with built-in cushioned workstations featuring LED lighting and electrical outlets. Here, people can plop down, open their laptops and do some quick work while they wait. Wood wall paneling and exposed wood beams accent the entire building's interior space. Music is constantly piped in.

Straight ahead is the lounge room. There is a wall-mounted big-screen television, beanbag chairs, as well as a comfortable black leather couch and chair. The orange- and coffee-painted walls boast a King Kong mural covering one entire wall and exposed brick on another. A massive and dramatic 23-light black metal chandelier dominates the room from above.

Down the hall on the left are glass windows encasing the building's conference room—which is dominated by a hefty wooden picnic table and wood benches all around. Green AstroTurf marks the floor. To engender creativity we have an orange-colored rear wall on which people can write during meetings with dry-erase markers. Another full wall displays a mural of trees and birds—it feels like you're in a park.

WE ARE BY NO MEANS DONE GROWING.

Directly across the hall is a break-room lounge stocked with all kinds of goodies—from every type of snack food you can think of to latte, French press, and espresso machines. In one corner stands a small library where staff can check out inspirational and motivational books.

The hall empties into a large two-story-tall room hosting SkySlope's support department, where employees support clients via live-chat, email and phones. There are stained concrete floors, exposed red brick, and wooden beams across the ceiling. Employees sit in comfortable high-backed leather swivel chairs in front of 20 black computer workstations placed on white-topped tables supported by red legs. They can write on the tabletops using dry-erase markers. Against one wall is a fully stocked refrigerator with an unlimited supply of energy drinks, as well as doorways to two executive offices. The stairway, with steps also featuring AstroTurf, leads up to the second floor. On the stairway wall, facing the support room, are comments excerpted from electronic surveys returned by subscribers at the end of support sessions:

"I love this guy!!! Y'all should probably give him a raise!!!"

"Kais [a support rep] deserves a 30-day paid vacation in Paris!"

"Jessica was Jonny on the spot and obviously a great GOOD LUCK CHARM."

We get 50+ comments like these every week.

Heading up the stairway, you pass photographs of employees from all SkySlope departments marking important milestones: The day a sales rep made a first closing. A support rep after his or her first positive feedback response. An activation specialist after the first complete launch of a company on SkySlope. In every instance, there is a color photo of the rep and a mounted piece of the person's tie (in the case of guys) that was cut off in celebration.

The spacious second floor is divided between the sales and activation departments. They labor at workstations set on tables built in against the walls that run the length and breadth of the room that was once used by an architectural firm. In lieu of carpeting we have more AstroTurf. Employees can write on these walls and railings with dry-erase markers. A large metal gong is rung when an account executive makes a sale. Helping to decorate the space are a dartboard, a pull-up bar, and a faux parking meter.

Construction is underway on another 3,000 square feet of the structure. The downstairs will feature more common areas with additional game tables. Upstairs we're planning an expansion of our growing activation and support departments.

Although we have expanded exponentially since 2009, we are by no means done growing. There is plenty more in store for this burgeoning company. Needless to say, SkySlope will be hiring more employees to help shoulder the additional workload. In fact, the company is having a hard time filling positions, in part due to a shortage of applicants we deem qualified.

To get an idea of the kind of people SkySlope is interested in hiring, take a look at an excerpt from one of our typical job postings.

DREAM JOB AVAILABLE:

Entrepreneurial Bad-Ass Who Believes Work/ Life Balance is a Crock

EVERYONE TALKS ABOUT WORK/LIFE BALANCE. But they've got it all wrong. Work and life aren't rivals. They're best buds, inseparable partners, and both inherently good.

We love Mondays, and we think everyone deserves a job where they do, too.

We believe that doing good work is an essential part of living a good life.

We're working on something new. We want you to be part of it.

WHERE IT STARTED

For five years we kids behind SkySlope have crusaded to make Real Estate Software fun. Our CEO was once the TOP Realtor® in the nation and needed this service for his company before it was an actual business.

WHY WE'RE DOING IT

Centuries ago, we wore uniforms and worked in factories. We clocked in, clocked out, and did what we were told.

Our work once fed our families, but not our souls. Not anymore.

You don't work in a factory. You decide what to work on, when to work, and how. You spend more of your life at work than ever before, form closer bonds with those you work with, and it's no longer rare for work to be a place you want to be.

But we still speak of work as a necessary evil. It's time we changed that.

We work because we love it.

SO WHAT IS IT?

Ever flipped through a business magazine and thought "Who are these people?!" Or walked into an office megastore only to encounter fluorescent lights, particle board, cheap chairs, and the faint scent of disappointment? We can do better.

Material will inspire and equip you to do your life's work.

We'll inspire with stories of our work heroes—from people who changed whole organizations from the inside, to companies experimenting with new ways to get things done and make life better, to one-man/woman shops traveling the globe and fashioning the life- and work-style of their dreams.

ABOUT THE JOB

What matters to us: Living and breathing our mission, passion for learning and doing, and strong internal drive.

YOUR RESPONSIBILITIES:

You know the joy of hard work. You crave responsibility, have an entrepreneurial bent, and want to learn how to create a new company from the beginning.

You're kick-ass, creative, and productive. (Also obsessive, decisive, and scrappy.) You finish what you start.

You're crazy organized. You've never seen: 1) a color-coded spreadsheet you didn't love; 2) a project you couldn't manage the hell out of; 3) a to-do you couldn't do. You're business-minded, social-media savvy, and have a knack for marketing.

You want a challenge. You may be young or old, experienced or green. But if you're ready to do, we're ready to teach, train, and help you grow.

Your work means the world to you. You couldn't have it any other way.

SkySlope is looking for hard workers. It's not as if we're searching for people who are this or that age or have this or that experience. We're looking for people who want to give it their all and learn a lot.

The 3,000-square-foot basement is accessed via a stairwell also carpeted in AstroTurf. It presently houses company Beach Cruiser bikes and electric scooters that staff are encouraged to take out a side door into the parking lot while on breaks, to pick up food or run errands. The basement will also be home to a full-length, fully equipped bowling alley to enhance employee enjoyment of our space.

We organize monthly staff parties around different themes. They usually celebrate the state where we have the most closed accounts that month. A while ago, we were down in Texas for a full month of training after landing a big account, and when the launch took place, we organized a Western-themed party. A caterer supplied all kinds of drinks and foods associated with Texas, from beans to ribs. The whole office was decked out with Texas-themed decorations. All the employees came to work that day in Texan or Western attire.

Employees get to invite their family members and friends as guests for these events. Sometimes we have upwards of 100 or 150 people.

These theme affairs also run the gamut from ugly sweater parties (where the staff wear old sweaters with deer heads embroidered on them, and the like) to holiday celebrations, to a black-and-white-tie VIP party where employees dress in formal wear.

The once-a-month themed parties follow our all-hands meeting with everyone in the office, which takes place the first Friday of every month. We call it the all-hands meeting because everyone is involved. We go over financials, cover updates from all the departments, brief people on what our subscribers are doing and saying, and what new SkySlope features are planned for the next quarterly release.

Our company tries to be very transparent. We want to make sure everyone knows about our new releases. And we also share a great many things with our staff. It can be very confidential, from the latest report on revenue brought in, to new subscriber accounts, to who's on top among our sales and support reps.

3
CHAPTER

GOING PAPERLESS

BUILT BY AGENTS FOR AGENTS

"SkySlope is the dramatic success it has become in a relatively short period of time, precisely because some of the most successful brokers and agents around the nation came together to create it out of a pressing need."

As a practicing real estate agent I originally created SkySlope for my own use, as well as for use by other agents. That's why SkySlope is unique among its competitors.

Another exclusive feature of SkySlope is our renowned support services department. Agents love it because they can—and do—turn to support reps 24/7, to help them use and understand the application and solve their specific problems. It doesn't matter what the problems are or what level of technical ability or experience the agents bring with them, our reps can help.

Realtors® derive multiple benefits from this platform. Take it from me, because I used to be one. People who don't have a background in real estate have created many of the platforms out there that compete with SkySlope. Some are title company people. Others are entrepreneurs who are technologically savvy and have just started dipping their toes into the real estate technology space. Some competitors are people who were in real estate but got out because they weren't all that successful at it—so they fashioned an online platform to help Realtors® be more successful. Hmmm. Detect any irony there?

SkySlope was created only after I was able to tap my extremely successful career in real estate, and I am constantly working with my colleagues to improve and refine it. The genesis of SkySlope was to fulfill a need I had as an agent: the growing burden of dealing with mountains of paperwork was interfering with my ability to get out there, drum up more business, and make more sales.

It started out as an aid just for agents. Later, we added systems that connect agents and brokers together. And we always tailor SkySlope to meet the unique processes and specific needs of each individual brokerage company that subscribes—so agents and brokers can interact seamlessly and much more efficiently, to their mutual benefit.

SkySlope is the dramatic success it has become in a relatively short period of time, precisely because some of the most successful brokers and agents around the nation came together to create it out of a pressing need. The agent side of SkySlope really developed when I began sharing the technology I created with some of the most successful agents and brokers in the country. They, in turn, began sharing their suggestions, many of which became—and continue to become—the next great SkySlope feature. Regular quarterly updates of improvements in SkySlope are issued to our subscribers; most of them are the result of continuous input from our brokers and their agents.

For example, one agent wanted to make sure SkySlope contained a reminder section, flagging task-specific events and milestones in the real estate transaction process, such as a reminder for agents to contact the buyer or seller to get him or her to sign the disclosure packet. That suggestion became an element of SkySlope in the subsequent release of new features.

THE RESULT OF CONTINUOUS INPUT FROM OUR BROKERS AND THEIR AGENTS.

Reminders can also cover referring buyers to loan representatives, showing appointments that have been set up with clients, and setting up all the various home inspections, whether for mold or termites, roofs or pools.

This suggestion process for new features is now being continued on a much larger scale. We discovered that soliciting and accepting recommendations only from the top producers at brokerage companies was very useful. However, many other agents we serve have good suggestions that top producers may not think of or utilize. So we have to take into consideration ideas from all agents who use our platform.

We did this on a small scale when there were only 40 people on our platform, even before it was named SkySlope. Agents could go on our forum and propose ideas, and all the other agents got to vote them up or down. Since then, we've taken this feedback suggestion model and scaled it nationally, making it available to our entire user base, resulting in the release of major new features every quarter. It has worked wonderfully.

Input from our uses has evolved our platform beyond what I originally imagined. It's our users—and not me—who are literally building SkySlope into the future. I take credit for founding and running the organization the way it is. Yet it is our users who guide our quarterly releases. They are the ones coming up with these innovations out of their practical day-to-day experiences with both real estate and SkySlope. They are the ones allowing us to build these exciting new features based on what works for them in their daily real estate practices.

The platform on the agent side started out with three core features: being able to create a listing, create a sale, and being able to review their closed files. Today, those core features incorporate a wide variety of fresh offerings, including triggers, digital signatures, and workflows—among many others.

Take digital or e-signatures. How many times do agents need to obtain their clients' signatures during the course of a normal real estate transaction? SkySlope eliminates the need for a client to go into the agent's office or for the agent to go to the client's home or business. We developed DigiSign™, SkySlope's e-signature platform. It lets agents send clients send documents electronically; clients can digitally sign and automatically return the files to the agents.

We're not the first to invent the digital signature and make it available. There are several such products on the market. But we crafted our own in-house e-signature product and made it available to our clients.

NO MORE TREKKING TO THE OFFICE TO DROP OFF OR PICK UP

When I was in my early 20s and just starting out in a real estate practice, I got bogged down with paperwork. I didn't know what was required of me as an agent, with all the different types of sales and listings. I had to learn about the documents and forms required by the law and my broker. It took a great deal of my time that could have been spent out in the field doing lead generation or buying and selling homes.

As I became a successful agent, I learned the drill very well: You went out and wrote up an offer for a client. You took the offer to the listing agent who accepted it. Then you had to drive into the office, make a copy of the offer and place it into your broker's in-basket. The broker reviewed the offer and the file, checked off what was missing and not missing, and returned a checklist to you. You went back to the office, picked up the checklist from your inbox and

SKYSLOPE USES A DIGITIZED COLOR CHECKLIST.

went out and obtained or completed anything missing, secured the requisite signatures, and took them back to the office to complete the checklist. That list was re-checked by the broker, who might have returned it to you if there were still necessary items to complete. Then the process repeated itself.

So, back then, the agent had to trek into the office and retrieve the checklist from the inbox. Or the broker could email the checklist, but the agent still had to go into the office to turn it back completed.

That laborious process began to change for me when I adopted the Microsoft SharePoint product that I customized for real estate. When I first developed my own platform, it was just for my own use through what I called Smith Premier, my corporation at the time. In those days, I still had to print everything out and submit it as a hard copy to my broker. But I used the platform because my staff and I wanted to easily and quickly access everything in one place. That's what eventually became SkySlope.

With SkySlope, the days are over when agents have to go into the office to turn in documents for compliance review by the broker. SkySlope uses a digitized color checklist that allows users to submit documents on the fly for compliance review through several different methods or forms such as email, fax, direct upload or digital signature. Agents can now turn in compliance review documents from the field while working on other tasks, or from home while they're relaxing and watching Jay Leno, or even while they're on vacation.

Busy real estate agents are always active. As a rule, they hate preparing and turning in paperwork to their brokers. Most of them aren't very good at it either. The successful ones are good at selling real estate, dealing one on one with clients, and serving their needs.

And they are good at negotiating—with dealers, buyers, and sellers, and other Realtors®. Those are their real talents.

Most agents who are good at paperwork are usually not so good at selling. I've not met many agents who are both superb at paperwork and great at selling too. Paperwork is just not in our blood. That's why many agents, as they become successful, hire on assistants, transaction coordinators, and administrators.

The seemingly endless world of paperwork that agents must deal with is all too familiar to every one of us. At any given time during a typical transaction, an agent may have to navigate an average of more than 60 forms or documents. It starts at the offer stage. Then there is the countering back and forth. It's great if you get your offer accepted in the first round, but multiple offers and counter-offers are not unusual, especially in the multi-offer market that we seem to be experiencing. Then there is the whole disclosure and inspection process. And finally there is the closing process.

This is why across the nation the ordinary transaction file totals 93 pages. Because of its greater volume of regulation, the normal transaction file in California goes to more than 200 pages. Oh, and that doesn't include homeowner association bylaws, and other rules and regulations that can easily double the size of the client's file.

Paperwork comes with the territory. It is dictated by government laws and rules, and by broker practices. It's part of what agents have to do to get paid. Yet that doesn't mean agents should be stuck with or bogged down in paper. Slogging through paperwork isn't the best use of their time. If you prioritize everything agents must do in their daily routines today, then spending time with their clients, prospecting for business, and performing lead generation should be at the top of their lists. You're only as good as the last deal you concluded. If you're stuck spending an inordinate amount of your time doing paperwork during the course of your transactions, that's

IT FREES AGENTS FROM THIS BURDEN THAT DOMINATES THEIR TIME AND IMPEDES THEIR SUCCESS.

not the best use of your time. If you are paying someone to do your paperwork or you can use an application that automates the process, as SkySlope does, you can focus your attention and efforts on selling and on generating new business that will produce more sales, which is the best use of your time.

How many times have I seen real estate agents literally carting around huge briefcases filled with folders, sometimes on wheels, because they need quick access to their most current files that are in the midst of being finalized? Some agents seem perpetually hunched over from carrying or lugging these mobile file cabinets. A client, broker or another agent calls with a concern or a question. "Oh, let me grab the folder," the overburdened agent will say. Or the agent has to respond, "Let me get back to the office to pick up the file."

SkySlope renders unnecessary all this carting about of paperwork, especially for agents who don't have their own staff to handle these affairs. It frees agents from this burden that dominates their time and impedes their success. It allows them to be on the go and out in the field, which is where they should be if they're going to make more money.

SkySlope even allows you to maneuver through this entire process using your mobile device or tablet, if need be. Or it can be done from a laptop or desktop computer. SkySlope is also unique insofar as we tailor our process to the specific needs of particular agents and brokers according to how they prefer to operate their businesses. We make SkySlope work for every kind of agent, whether he or she is a single agent, an agent belonging to a team, or an agent who uses an assistant or transaction coordinator. It doesn't matter.

Real estate agents can turn to SkySlope every day of the week and at any hour of the day or night. Say it's a weekend or in the evening. An agent's client wants to see a document—maybe a copy of an inspection report—or has a question that requires the agent to examine a document in the transaction file. The agent needs to respond in a timely manner. SkySlope enables the agent to do so immediately and with no more effort than it takes to make a few clicks on a mobile device.

Realtors® are also always on the go. They don't have the time to deal with paperwork. All brokers will agree their agents should not be spending their time concentrating on the ABCs of bureaucracy. That's the job of administrators or assistants. For agents who don't have that kind of assistance—and 99 percent don't—the agents get stuck doing the paperwork themselves. They have to do it. There is no alternative. It's required by the law and by their brokers.

SUPPORT SERVICES COMMENTS:

'Above and beyond truly is your default setting'

The following are just a small sampling of the hundreds of comments SkySlope's support staff receive every month from agents and brokers.

"Quickly answered my question."

Gene Fennelly, *Allison James Estates and Homes*

"Everyone at SkySlope support is always very helpful and kind. Thank you!"

Lisa Layman, *John. L. Scott Realty*

"Kais was prompt and took care of the issue right away!"

Linda McKiernan, *McKiernan Realty*

"Your customer service is excellent. No matter the time of day or day of the week you get back with an answer within minutes. SkySlope is a great program, saves me so much time and money plus it helps me get the job done correctly and quickly. Great company and service. Big Thanks!"

Bruce Gasparre, *Southern Homes of The Carolinas*

"Kais was excellent to work with and resolved the problem quickly!"

Barry Ward, *Barry Ward Realty*

"Thank you, John, for [the] communication with my client and rescuing my offer."

Kathy Kampman, *RE/MAX Realty Centre*

"Awesome support team!"

Sheila Pace, *Troop Real Estate, Inc.*

"John was awesome! A great help!"

Chamise Johnson, *Realty World Selzer Realty*

"Great support. Thank you so much."

Lisa Gross, *Balistreri Realty*

"John was very helpful! I know when I contact support, I will get my issue resolved. Thanks!"

Traci Komenda, *Team Patterson Realty*

"John looked like a funny guy in his photo, and the fact that he solved the problem made me laugh at how easy it was. Funny guy who can solve problems = satisfied customer."

Jonathan Flores,
Briggs Freeman Sotheby's International Realty

"Awesome! Kais was quick to solve my problem and I'm very thankful that he was able to move the transaction to our office side and delete the trial account that our agent created, therefore less confusion in the future. Keep up the great job. Thanks again for the help!"

Tina Marie del Mundo, *Century 21 Realty Alliance*

"My issue was taken care of ASAP…thanks"

Stephen Ferrebee, *Northwood Realty Services*

"Good, very quick response. I am very satisfied!"

Lily Sie, *RE/MAX 2000 Realty*

"Ashley was amazing, easy to talk to, fast response to my error, kind, understanding and very professional. Thank you! Thank you! Kais for your help."

Kathy Bartle, *Legacy Real Estate & Associates*

"Excellent! Not only did he fix the problem for me, he told me what was wrong so I won't have the problem again."

Debbie Copeland, *RE/MAX Trinity*

"Your support is always very good."

Karen Mezzetta, *Home Quest Realty*

"John always comes through when I have a tough question."

Jeff Green, *Allison James Estates and Homes*

"SkySlope support is the best ever!"

Barbara Mallord, *Century 21 M&M and Associates*

"The response email I got was easy to understand and solved my problem right away:). Thank you!"

Shannon Buha, *Northwood Realty Services*

"SkySlope is yet another amazing 'foot forward' toward technology in going paperless and efficiently managing your real estate transactions. In this fast-paced, ever-changing environment, this type of technology is not a 'want' but a 'need.' In addition, their Customer Support team is amazing. Ashley was amazing, professional in her responses, quick to answer the phone and very amiable and friendly. Since I am a new engager of this service, I had also just spoken to John prior to Ashley and I can tell you that he was wonderful as well and right on the mark. SkySlope is the answer and an amazing benefit for any agent who has the privilege to be engaged in utilizing it."

Bryan L. Garrity, *J.D., The Garrity Group*

"Excellent customer service, thank you for the great support :)"

Cristina Velasco, *Century 21 M&M and Associates*

"Excellent attention towards making sure that I understood the task at hand. Was very clear on his explanations."

Melba Muniz, *Balistreri Realty*

"I'm so glad Ashley took the time to go into my computer. She was able to figure out a very simple solution [so] I will recognize the problem next time and be able to handle it myself. Thanks Ashley!"

Camille Marshall, *Southern Homes of The Carolinas*

"I don't know specifically how you guys do it, but you must have an amazing company culture/training method. I came to this job from 26 years in retail management and I have NEVER seen consistent customer service the way you guys do it (and I'd always thought my own staff was pretty darn good). Above and beyond truly is your default setting."

Nancy Wolf, *Gardner Realtors®*

"Got the answer to my question quickly."

Jo Ann O'Fallon, *Allison James Estates and Homes*

"The support was fast, knowledgeable and courteous."

Belladonna Riso, *Solstice Realty*

"It's Painless to Go Paperless."

Tracy Brown, *Allison James Estates and Homes*

"When I started using SkySlope I felt that this was a file management tool that was created by a team of Realtors® because it provided everything we need on a daily basis. To make things even better, the company provided awesome 24/7 customer service. This combined makes SkySlope the best tool with access to my files anywhere in the world. It also allows my manager to review every file for accuracy and catch and comment on any mistake or missing documents. This gives me peace of mind in my business.

In New Jersey, we were severely affected by Super Storm Sandy. One of the real estate brokers in our state lost most of its transaction paper files, which became a disaster for the agents.
With SkySlope, all of the documents in every file are uploaded and protected from disaster loss. SkySlope is user friendly and fun to use. [It] almost seems magic the way it works. I applaud founder and CEO Tyler Smith for his efforts in producing an invaluable program for every Realtor®."

Wayne Zelenak, *Richard A. Weidel Realtors®*

MAKING IT EASIER FOR AGENTS TO RESPOND

Agents work hard, but they shouldn't be slaves to their practices. Nevertheless, agents all know the reality: If someone—particularly a client—calls and wants something, you jump. The best Realtors® certainly negotiate the best deals and satisfy their clients' basic needs. But real estate agents also live and survive on referrals, and the top brokers and agents across the country run their successful businesses based on referrals.

Quick responses when clients have questions or worries aren't as important as closing deals to the clients' satisfaction. But they are an important way clients measure agents' effectiveness and responsiveness. (Buffini and Company, the number one coaching and training firm for real estate agents in North America, which I once used, developed elaborate systems and a curriculum for helping boost referral business for Realtors®. Take a look at: www.buffiniandcompany.com.)

Success isn't just about doing a good job for your clients. It's also about the clients' perception of you as someone who is responsive to them. And that frequently comes down to how you perform when it comes to the little things.

In my quest for more referrals, I always went above and beyond as an agent. Most Realtors® give closing gifts: A $100 bottle of fine wine or a fancy cheese platter. I had 32 items—all extras—from which I could choose to provide as part of each deal. No one else I knew was doing what I did. I did it because I worked, and succeeded, as an agent through referrals.

I'd write personal notes and send them to my clients—30 of them a week. Many of them were unique.

"We're interviewing other agents," a prospective client would say at the end of our first meeting. So I'd write in my note, "Great meeting you. I'd love to represent you." Except, instead of my note arriving as a card in the mail with a first-class stamp affixed, my personal card arrived via Federal Express because it was the size of the front door of a house. "Honey, did we order a closet?" the spouse would ask. Now, that got noticed.

I would get the client the best lender who would supply the best terms possible. Later, when word arrived that the loan had been approved, I'd stop by my client's office and drop off a small bottle of good chilled Champagne. My card would read, "Congratulations on the loan." They'd open up the cold bottle of Champagne or at least show it off to all their co-workers. "Where'd that come from?" someone would inevitably ask.

"Oh, it's from my Realtor®, Tyler Smith," would be the response.

On move-in day, I'd have a pizza delivered so the family would have food when they arrived at their new residence. Even though I had a pizza guy deliver the pizza, the box it came in didn't say Pizza Hut or Round Table. It was a jumbo-sized stylized Tyler Smith pizza box with a big picture of me wearing a chef's hat. It was all about marketing and making impressions.

I used to teach a class for agents on how to effectively work by referral. It was about how to get a guaranteed two referrals out of every deal they closed. Most agents do things after the fact. I did things differently. For example, you notice a new car that crosses your path when you've just purchased a new car. If you're in the process of buying a house, when's the best time to work on getting a referral? Most agents will do their marketing after the closing. I did my marketing before, during, and after—all three!

We're operating in a demanding real estate market, and there are usually a number of agents from whom buyers or sellers can choose. Sure, people buy cars, TV sets, and major appliances all the time. But clients have a lot on the line when they're buying or selling their homes, since we're handling what is normally the biggest single financial purchase and investment they will ever make in their lives. They can be buying or selling homes worth hundreds of thousands of dollars—sometimes $500,000 or more. That's a lot of money. So they expect us to be constantly available and on top of our game all of the time. Real estate agents have to always be accessible at all hours, and always be "on." They don't turn off their phones.

SkySlope doesn't change that reality. It does make it a lot easier for agents to respond and keep their clients happy, but do it in a way that also helps preserve the time they get to spend outside of work.

COMPANIES THAT THINK THEY'RE PAPERLESS, BUT AREN'T

What if a real estate operation is already paperless?

That happens. SkySlope's sales team approaches a company; "We're already paperless," they tell us.

Most of these firms think they are paperless, but they're truly not. We discover that fact by digging in and learning their processes. The competing paperless platforms they may use don't offer any way for users to retrieve documents electronically. We do, through a patent-pending process.

Take, for instance, one very large real estate brokerage firm in California we encountered. It had 1,000 agents. These agents still had to bring in their paperwork, turn it in and have administrators scan the paper into their "paperless" system. With SkySlope, agents quickly and easily upload their own documents so administrators just have to audit everything in the cloud. There are no more file counters. No more file cabinets stuffed with materials from transaction files. There are no more paper folders at all—and no more sticky notes, labels, pins or clamps. They're all gone.

There are also no more inefficiencies. There are no more agents telling brokers, "I turned in that document and you lost it." There are no more brokers telling agents, "You didn't put it on my desk." All those problems—and excuses—have been eliminated.

Our SkySlope sales staff will call up, saying they're doing a survey. "Are you paperless?" we will ask.

"Yes," is the answer. But when we probe just a little deeper we—and the company we're talking to—soon discover it uses some methods and practices that are paperless, but the firm is not really paperless. Agents still must bring in hard copy paperwork to brokers who then upload the documents. What many of them are doing is replacing their file cabinet systems at the office with a paperless system only after closings, after the deals are done. SkySlope makes everything paperless from start to finish.

The client signs a document using our own DigiSign™ e-signature. The paper doesn't need to be scanned or input. It's signed and exists as soft copy. It's now in the cloud.

What's more, the agent no longer has to bring the document to where the clients are, get them to sign it, take it back to the broker's office and hand it over to the auditor or administrator who then puts it in a file. Instead, the client signs it electronically and it's instantaneously placed in a file in the cloud where any authorized person—agent or broker—can access it.

And this can all be done from a mobile device.

Many real estate companies also think they are paperless,

but they are not, just because too many agents find the paperless platforms too hard to use or they're afraid of the technology—or of change itself. Most agents hate change.

The average age of real estate agents today is 57 years old. They didn't grow up with computers or advanced technology. When they began their careers in the business 25 or 30 or 40 years ago, they didn't have the multiple listing service (MLS). If you wanted to buy a house from a Realtor® 30 years ago, the agent would ask, "What are you looking for?"

When you answered, "A three-bedroom, two-bath house in this neighborhood," the agent would pull out his or her handy book of hard copy listings and skim through it, searching for appropriate properties.

Now the industry is all about technology. Successful agents are forced to learn how to use it. It can be tough for a number of reasons. Not the least of those reasons is that clients are often the so-called Eco Boomers or Millennials—20- or 30-something-year-olds, the largest generation in American history since the Baby Boomers. There were maybe 80 million Millennials born between 1982 and 1995.

Guess what they want to use? Technology. Their whole lives are built around it. When it comes to real estate, they want to peruse online listings. They want to e-sign documents. They want to be paperless. They don't want to face a fat transaction file that reminds them of what they have to do once a year at tax time.

A lot of resistance to paperless platforms is rooted in a person's age or generation. Yet today's agents need tools to accomplish what their clients demand; those tools are frequently technological. If agents don't deliver, they will fail. There are plenty of competitors out there who are trying to provide what their clients want.

Several years ago I got a memorable call from a seller who

also wanted to look at a house. I had a listing coordinator and staff who usually handled these tasks. But I decided to do this one myself. I put the whole presentation for this potential client on an iPad. The client said, "I'm interviewing seven agents."

NOW THE INDUSTRY IS ALL ABOUT TECHNOLOGY.

"Well, you saved the best for last," I responded confidently. "Let's get started."

"Do you have a book, a comparative market analysis comp sheet?" he asked, when he saw that I'd arrived empty-handed. He had six with him, all stacked up and in a nice bound book, a presentation from another Realtor®, who, he said, "is so great with all the comparables."

"You need a paperweight for that?" I asked as I pulled out my device. "This is what we call an iPad. I'm going to do my presentation on it for you, but I didn't have to kill a tree to make this presentation."

He looked at me skeptically.

"No one's done this for you?" I asked.

"No."

"I know technology. I'm probably the youngest person you've interviewed?"

"Yes," he replied. This guy was playing hardball with me.

"Take the six other agents you interviewed," I said. "Go ask them how many homes they sold in the last six months. I promise you I sold more during that time than all of them put together. And I don't have big fancy bound presentations for you. Mine's on an iPad."

I showed him the comps online. He objected: "What about this property that the other agent pulled up? Why don't you have this one?"

"Because it's in a different subdivision," I answered.

"No, it's not."

"Yes, it is. Let's pull it up." I had the Internet at my fingertips, so I pulled it up and showed it to him. He and the other agent were wrong. The property was outside the area he wanted.

So who looked like the pro? Here I was, this young guy who had sold a lot of real estate and wasn't afraid to respectfully call the client out. You have to be ready to do that if you're a top-producing agent. And I could prove my point with data that was immediately accessible with a few clicks on the iPad.

If I had gone into the presentation with paper, I would have been just like the competition. And he might not have chosen me. Or he might have wanted to overprice his house to a point where it wouldn't have sold. Without the wealth of data available on my iPad, he might have insisted on listing his property 15 percent higher than its worth instead of what it should have gone for—and what he did list it for because he hired me. That would have made him mad, since he wanted to sell his house and move into the new home very quickly.

I liked to price my homes just a little below market to create urgency and to attract multiple offers. It's a strategy that gets the blood flowing and the bodies there. People hired me because I negotiated so well. I'd negotiate to get $1 more. It was not about the money.

We received multiple offers. I sent back the standard counter-offer addendum I prepared in every multiple offer scenario. Then I called the buyer's agent. My message went something like this:

> *Thanks so much for the offer. I appreciate it. And thanks for showing the property. We're in a multiple-offer counter situation. I know your client wants the property. However, there is a lot of traction on this house—multiple offers. So Mr. Buyer's Agent, you need to go back to your clients, see how*

badly they want this home, and offer 'X' dollars more in order to get it. If you don't, that's fine. But I've done my research: There is only one other home on the market in the area like this one and it has multiple offers as well.

So I'd like to strike a deal today. But your buyers will have to come up a little. Contact them and get back to me.

• • •

That always worked. I was like a bulldog. That's what I loved to do. Depending on the year and the market—buyer's or seller's, and whether the market was decent, even though I priced my homes a little below market, I usually ended up getting more because we'd get into multiple offer situations. The number one thing I told my sellers was that if they listened to me—and priced their homes right—I'd get them what they were asking for.

My client in this case was delighted that I sold his house so quickly and got him a good price.

IT'S PAINLESS TO GO PAPERLESS

That's what one Realtor® commented after dealing with support reps from SkySlope. Think about real estate agents and who they really are. Imagine the typical independent contractor. I haven't worked for someone else—I haven't been in that box—since I was 20 years of age, before launching my career in real estate. Since then, I've been a 1099 independent contractor or I've run my own companies. I can't imagine working for someone else now; I'm too opinionated. It's not that I'm averse to listening to what others have to say. I just like to feel free to speak my mind—and so do about 90 percent of the Realtors® I've known over the years. They're free spirits and they're very independent-minded. They expect to go the extra mile for their clients. That's also what they look for in the brokers with whom they choose to associate.

In their minds, agents are the straw that stirs the drink. That's just how it is with them.

That is also why real estate agents who want to succeed need SkySlope to compete in our very competitive, technologically-driven world. That's also a fact.

SkySlope is so easy to learn and so easy to use that anyone can do it. Once agents are exposed to the platform and the considerable time and money it saves them, even those who are the least technologically savvy and the most resistant to change never want to go back to having to deal with a paper document system. SkySlope provides our clients with hands-on training and a state-of-the-art technical support staff that is available 24/7, whenever agents or brokers have questions or need help using the platform or solving any problem that occurs.

What's great about SkySlope for the agents? It is the most user-friendly platform on the market.

There is zero room for error in our business these days. There really are no choices when it comes to whether or not to use an online transaction management platform. And there are really no choices about which platform to select.

Agents and brokers built SkySlope…for agents and brokers.

ABOUT TYLER SMITH

A native of Sacramento, California, Tyler Smith grew up in the city's suburbs and discovered an early love of working and being independent. He began as a bus boy at a family-owned restaurant near his home at the age of 13. To earn money to buy his first car at 16, Tyler went to work at the local Target department store, quickly rising to become one of the company's youngest front-end managers at the age of 18.

He bought his first house at age 20, and soon decided to get into real estate. He took classes to study for the state real estate examination, passed it and became associated with a local brokerage company. After initially only selling several homes a year, Tyler attended a big multi-day retreat offered by prominent real estate coach and trainer Brian Buffini. Tyler was so impressed with what he saw that he paid for a full year's worth of coaching and training with the organization.

Within three months, Tyler began to see his business take off.

That year, he closed 13 real estate transactions. Then he tripled his business each year after that.

He hired an assistant at the recommendation of his real estate coach, who knew how well Tyler responds to pressure. Tyler's practice grew even more. He and his team of assistants and coordinators were selling 264 homes a year by 2009.

Yet Tyler was confronted by a mountain of paperwork that grew bigger and bigger the more successful he became. He knew it was inhibiting his success.

That's what drove Tyler to experiment with all the available transaction management products. None of them, which were designed by people from outside the real estate industry, met his needs as a practicing Realtor®. So he decided to fashion his own online platform, which eventually became SkySlope.

Today, Tyler Smith devotes his full-time efforts to running and constantly growing SkySlope, which now boasts more than 40 full-time employees—the best and the brightest in both the tech and real estate worlds—at its headquarters in downtown Sacramento. SkySlope, which now serves subscribers across the United States and Canada, dramatically outshines its competition because it is a paperless platform designed by a real estate agent to meet the unique needs of real estate agents and brokers.

Published by SkySlope Publishing

Second Printing January 2015
ISBN: 978-1-63068-005-3

Printed in the United States of America
10 9 8 7 6 5 4 3 2

Library of Congress Control Number (LCCN): 2013919517